Sandra
Scott

BETTE DAVIS

BETTE DAVIS

A BIOGRAPHY IN PHOTOGRAPHS

A JAMES SPADA ASSOCIATES BOOK

by
CHRISTOPHER NICKENS

A DOLPHIN BOOK
Doubleday & Company, Inc.
Garden City, New York
1985

BOOKS BY CHRISTOPHER NICKENS
Bette Davis: A Biography in Photographs
Elizabeth Taylor: A Biography in Photographs
IN COLLABORATION
Streisand: The Woman and the Legend
(with James Spada)
The Telephone Book
(with Gregory Rice)
ILLUSTRATIONS ONLY
Voices From Home
(by Anne Francis)

ACKNOWLEDGMENTS

For their invaluable help in the preparation of this book, I am extremely grateful
to George Zeno, Michel Parenteau, Robert Scott, Karen Swenson, Lester Glassner,
Michael Hawks, Phillip Castanza, Gregory Rice, Joel Kudler, Frank Teti, Ken de Bie,
and Mary Barton. A special thank you is, once again, due Stuart Timmons and the
helpful staff of the Academy of Motion Picture Arts and Sciences library.

I am also appreciative of the kind encouragement of
Paul O'Driscoll, Jerry Clar, Richard Parker, Bruce R. Mandes, Vernon Patterson,
Guy Vespoint, Judy Flaherty Spinner, Michael Minor, Bob Greene, John Cusimano,
Lance Benware, Kathy Robbins, Laura Van Wormer, Nell Hanson and Paul Bresnick.

DESIGNED BY KEN de BIE

Library of Congress Cataloging in Publication Data

Nickens, Christopher.
  Bette Davis, a biography in photographs.

    "A James Spada Associates book."

    "A Dolphin book."

  1. Davis, Bette, 1908-   —Portraits, etc.

        I. Title.
PN2287.D32N5 1985   791.43'028'0924 [B]   84-22279
        ISBN 0-385-19675-X

PRINTED IN THE UNITED STATES OF AMERICA
FIRST EDITION

In honor of women everywhere
who, like Bette Davis,
have struggled.

CONTENTS

INTRODUCTION

BEFORE HOLLYWOOD

Bette Davis may never have embarked on her magnificent career if, as a child, she had been exposed to a warm, loving relationship between her mother and father. She once said, "I cannot recall *one* moment of affection between my parents in our home." Bette's observations of the starchy relations between her parents made her skeptical about marriage and helped her to choose a career in acting instead of the domestic life expected of young women of her generation.

She was born Ruth Elizabeth Davis in Lowell, Massachusetts on April 5, 1908. Her arrival in the first year of her parents' marriage was unplanned and unwanted by her father, who reportedly suggested she be given up for adoption because he felt that starting a family would impede his career as a law student. By all accounts, Harlow Morrell Davis was a stern, insensitive autocrat who considered fatherhood nothing more than a necessary evil. He never physically abused his daughter, but neither was he moved when Betty (as she was nicknamed) uttered

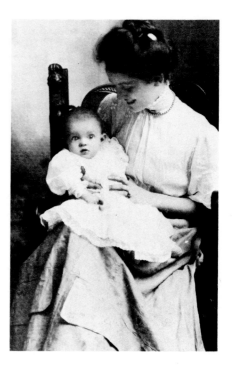

ABOVE: In this pose with her mother, Bette was less than six months old, but she was already flashing the large, compelling eyes that would later become familiar to moviegoers all over the world.

LEFT: At three, Bette takes the reins in this study with her father. In her 1962 autobiography, Davis recalled a typical example of Harlow Davis' Victorian methods of child rearing: "Daddy believed that children should not sit at the dining table with grownups until they were able to conduct an intelligent conversation. We *were* allowed to have dinner on Sundays, however, with the family."

OPPOSITE: In 1914, Bette (right) and her younger sister Bobby model matching outfits beside the family car.

"Papa" as her first word.

In great contrast, Betty's mother Ruthie Favor Davis was an energetic woman of keen intelligence who excelled at painting, public speaking and photography. She must have been somewhat of a maverick in turn-of-the-century New England, and one might wonder what she ever saw in Harlow Davis.

Betty worshipped her mother from the beginning, and later compared her to a painting by John Singer Sargent and to Jo Marsh, the spunky heroine of *Little Women*. Ruthie in turn adored her daughter; she instilled in her a love of the arts and encouraged her individuality. Symbolic of this was Ruthie's decision to change the spelling of Betty to Bette at the suggestion of a family friend who had just read Balzac's *Cousin Bette*.

When Bette was eighteen months old, she was joined by her sister Barbara. Bobby, as she was nicknamed, became a welcome playmate for Bette, though her birth did nothing to bring her constantly warring parents closer together; they divorced in 1918. Ten-year-old Bette reacted to the split with mixed emotions. She had always tried to please her father and she would miss him. On the other hand, she felt freed from his stifling authoritarianism. Years later, Davis remembered that she responded to the news of her parents' divorce with an amusing non sequitur: "Now we can go on a picnic and have a baby."

A short time after the divorce, Bette and Bobby were enrolled in a rural boarding school to enable Ruthie to take a job as a governess in Manhattan. This was the beginning of several years of odd jobs Ruthie needed to supplement Harlow's alimony payments, and dozens of relocations for her daughters. Ruthie once estimated that the Davis family moved a remarkable *eighty* times in less than seven years.

Bette enjoyed her school years, but didn't give much thought to her future until, barely into her teens, she attended a performance in Boston of Ibsen's *The Wild Duck*, starring the legendary Blanche Yurka. Years later, Davis recalled the impact the production had on her: "I had never seen Ibsen before and I was fascinated by his power of characterization and the magnificence of his brooding emotion. It was my first serious theater and a whole new world opened up to me." Indeed, the minute she left the theater Bette proudly announced to a startled Ruthie and Bobby that she had found her calling: she would become an actress.

BELOW: A sixteen-year-old Bette (in knickers) and Bobby are photographed on the grounds of the Cushing Academy in Massachusetts, a school Ruthie chose for them because she had enjoyed going there as a young girl. Bette was a good student, with particular talents for history and languages as well as a love for tennis. It was at Cushing that she experienced her first romance—with a young music student, Harmon "Ham" Nelson, Jr., who would drift in and out of Bette's life for several years before becoming her first husband.

TOP OPPOSITE: Bette spent her summers away from Cushing at the Mariarden Dance School in New Hampshire. Through the school's curriculum, Davis acquired a physical grace that was the foundation of her self-confidence as an aspiring actress. Her first public exposure was as a dancing fairie in *A Midsummer Night's Dream*, but she soon graduated to a solo turn in a popular interpretive dance of the day, *The Moth* (pictured). Recalling the dance years later, Bette said, "I remember the excitement of performing that night in front of an audience—the applause thrilled me. I recall (Ruthie and Bobby) looking at me afterwards as if they'd never seen me before."

Indeed, Bette's success that summer made Ruthie realize that her daughter's desire for a theatrical career was not just a teenage fantasy.

From this point on, all of the resources of the Davis family would be thrown unequivocally behind Bette's ambitions.

BOTTOM RIGHT: Bette is pensive in her 1925 Cushing graduation portrait—taken by Ruthie. Her senior year was an active one; she helped finance it by working as a waitress, acted the lead in the senior play, and was voted the prettiest girl in the class. She saw less of Ham Nelson (he had transferred to another school), and although he returned to escort Bette to her graduation dance, it was a bittersweet evening for her. "When we said goodnight, we both felt it was an end of something—a parting of the ways, perhaps."

Following her graduation, Bette spent a carefree summer with Ruthie and Bobby in Maine, then moved to Manhattan to pursue an acting career. The first drama school she applied to was under the tutelage of the celebrated actress Eva Le Gallienne. Unfortunately, Bette's self confidence suffered a serious setback when Le Gallienne (following a disastrous "cold" reading during which Bette giggled nervously) told Davis, "I can see that your attitude toward the theater is not sincere enough to warrant my taking you as a pupil."

Although heartbroken by the rejection, Bette followed Ruthie's advice and immediately applied at the highly-respected John Murray Anderson-Robert Milton Dramatic School. She was accepted, and went on to win two scholarships during her three-year stay at the school. Her diction instructor during this time was the renowned actor George Arliss, and she studied dance with Martha Graham, who said of her, "She had control, discipline...electricity. I knew she would be something."

RIGHT: In 1929, Bette makes her New York stage debut opposite Grover Burgess in *The Earth Between*, a controversial play about incest on a Nebraska farm. Davis received fine reviews for this Greenwich Village production; she was called "entrancing" by the *Times* and credited with "true emotional insight" by the *World*. It was a small-scale triumph, but one which Bette had worked doggedly for.

Her summers away from the Anderson-Milton school were spent gathering experience in several small production companies, most notably the George Cukor Repertory group in Rochester. She appeared successfully in over eight plays, in roles of varying size and type—she eagerly accepted any acting challenge. But her obsessive approach to her work left little time for socializing, and many of the other company members considered her a snob. Eventually she was fired by Cukor, who felt that she didn't fit in with the repertory concept. Shortly thereafter, Bette agreed to return to New York and join the production of *The Earth Between*. Its success gave her renewed hope—and more importantly, several choice job offers.

OPPOSITE: A publicity montage for *Broken Dishes*, the domestic comedy that brought Bette her strongest New York exposure when it opened on Broadway in November, 1929. She had spent most of the year touring in two Ibsen plays including *The Wild Duck* with Blanche Yurka—the star and the play which, just a few years earlier, had inspired Bette to pursue an acting career.

It was during the run of *Broken Dishes* that Davis was first approached about acting in motion pictures. She agreed to a screen test for Samuel Goldwyn. Unfortunately, little care was taken with Bette's wardrobe, makeup or lighting at Paramount's Long Island studio, and the test was not a success. Supposedly, when Goldwyn ran the film in Hollywood he yelled, "Who did this to me?" The role (in *The Devil To Pay*) was given to Myrna Loy, but Davis was philosophical about the experience. She knew the test had been dreadful, and she had little interest in films, with her theater career taking firm root.

Following *Broken Dishes*, Bette appeared in the road company of the show until she was called back to

New York to replace the ingenue in *Solid South*. The show lasted only thirty-one performances, but it brought Bette her second screen test.

This one—for Universal—was successful, and the studio offered Bette the lead in *Strictly Dishonorable*, based on the Preston Sturgess play, to begin filming in just two months. Within a few days, Bette had signed a contract and she and Ruthie were on their way to California. Davis thought her stay in Los Angeles would be temporary, but it was over twenty years before she would act on the New York stage again.

THE
THIRTIES

OPPOSITE: December 13, 1930: Bette and Ruthie pose at the Plaza Hotel after arriving in Hollywood. A Universal representative was sent to meet their train, but he returned to the studio empty handed, reporting that he had seen no one who resembled a young contract actress. When told of the unintentional snub Davis remarked, "I had a dog with me–you should have known I was an actress!" Things did not improve during Bette's first few days at the studio. In the Hollywood tradition it was suggested that she change her name–to Bettina Dawes. She flatly refused: "I will not go through life known as Between the Drawers."

LEFT: Bette looks forlorn in her first film, *Bad Sister*, released in March 1931. Shortly after her arrival at Universal, studio chief Carl Laemmle decided that she lacked the sex appeal required for *Strictly Dishonorable*. Disappointed, Davis spent her first few weeks sitting for portrait sessions and testing with other young actors until she was cast in the smallish role of the *good* sister in *Bad Sister*, starring Conrad Nagel. *Variety* said of Bette's first screen appearance: "...holds much promise in her handling of Laura, sweet, simple and the very essence of repression." The New York *Times*, however, called her work "lugubrious."

Bette's inexperience with the ways of Hollywood caused her some embarrassment during one scene. She was supposed to change the diaper of a baby girl, but discovered to her great chagrin that the child was actually a boy, a common practice in Hollywood with children too young to be differentiated on screen. Her deep blush is apparent even on black and white film.

OPPOSITE: Although dressed plainly for her first few film roles, Bette was encouraged to "doll-up" for publicity photos such as this one. She had always been considered more than attractive enough for her stage career, but once she encountered Hollywood's narrow concept of beauty she became extremely sensitive about her looks. Davis felt unequipped to convey the lacquered glamour of the day, and envied the likes of Greta Garbo—her favorite movie actress—and Jean Harlow, who became a close friend. Bette's self-consciousness was not helped any when she learned that the Universal brass had nicknamed her "the little brown wren."

RIGHT: A portrait taken during the shooting of Bette's second film, *Seed*, had nothing to do with her role as the wholesome daughter of John Boles. Her part was so small she

wasn't mentioned in advertising copy or in reviews of the picture. Davis' displeasure with Universal's handling of her fledgling career was tempered somewhat by the revival of her romance with Ham Nelson, who visited her during the *Seed* filming.

LEFT: Davis' final appearance for Universal in 1931 was in the moody romantic drama *Waterloo Bridge*, a starring vehicle for Mae Clark. Again, Bette's role was small and little notice was taken of her in reviews. She despaired of ever establishing a decent film career, and was not encouraged when she heard that, after viewing *Waterloo Bridge*, Carl Laemmle had commented, "Her sex appeal simply ain't. No man could ever be interested in her!" Not surprisingly, the studio was more than happy to "loan" Davis out—at a profit—to RKO when that studio requested her services for a big-budgeted production, *Other People's Business*.

14

BELOW: Immediately following completion of *The Menace*, Bette was rushed into another loan-out—to Capitol Films for *Hell's House*, a reform school melodrama filmed in less than two weeks. Bette enjoyed working with Pat O'Brien (pictured) for the first time, but she knew the film was a bomb, and was not surprised when Universal decided against renewing her $450-a-week contract.

Devastated at the thought of returning to New York as a failure, Bette and Ruthie began packing for the trip home. But in the tradition of the popular cliffhangers of the day, Bette was rescued in the nick of time by George Arliss, who not only kept his promise of an interview, but cast Davis in *The Man Who Played God*. It was a big break in an important picture, and Bette couldn't wait for filming to begin at Warner Brothers.

OPPOSITE: Frank Albertson and Bette were the young lovers in *Way Back Home*, the final title given to *Other People's Business*, released by RKO in 1932. The film was not a success, despite the large budget and location filming, but it afforded Bette her most important role to date. It was also the first film in which she was photographed to good advantage. She told biographer Whitney Stine, "This is the first encouragement I had had, as to my face on the screen." For the first time since leaving New York, Bette felt hopeful about her future in motion pictures.

ABOVE: Unfortunately, Bette's hopes were dimmed again when Universal lent her to Columbia for *The Menace*, an implausible murder mystery filmed in eight days. (Bette is shown here with Walter Byron.) In another tiny part, Davis went essentially unnoticed by the public and the press. In an indirect way, however, this film provided her with a contact that would give her career the boost it sorely needed.

One of the supporting players in *The Menace*, Murray Kinnel, was impressed with Bette and mentioned her to his good friend George Arliss, who was looking for a young actress to cast in his next film. In the years since Arliss had taught Bette elocution at the Anderson-Milton school, he had become one of Hollywood's most prestigious actors—winning an Oscar for his first sound film *Disraeli* in 1929. He promised Kinnel that he would set up an interview for Bette.

The Man Who Played God tells the sentimental story of a concert pianist (Arliss, pictured) who suddenly loses his hearing, learns to read lips, and in the process decides to help strangers with financial gifts. As his forty-years-younger fiancee, Bette stands by him through all of this, but eventually ends up in love with another man at Arliss' encouragement. Arliss had filmed a silent version of the story in 1922, and it would be revived again in 1955 as *Sincerely Yours*, a vehicle for Liberace.

Although Bette was admiring of Arliss, she was not overwhelmed by his stature, nor was she outwardly intimidated about working at a new studio under the scrutiny of Jack Warner—who was considering putting her under long-term contract. Davis approached her role with great confidence as the result of two important factors: she was completely prepared as an actress, and she finally felt comfortable with her image on screen—thanks to Warner's famed makeup expert Perc Westmore. He convinced Bette to lighten her hair from her natural ash blonde, which had always photographed as mousey brown on screen. He was also the first makeup artist to analyze her features to determine how best to highlight her face for the camera. Davis was deeply appreciative of his efforts: "...for the first time I really looked like myself. It was for me a new lease on life. As a matter of fact I was compared to Constance Bennett. I was very flattered."

Bette's performance in *The Man Who Played God* surprised and delighted Arliss, who wrote in his autobiography, "I knew she had a nice little part...so I hoped for the best. I did not expect anything but a nice little performance. But she startled me; the nice little part became a deep and vivid creation; this young girl had been able to discover and portray something that my imagination had failed to conceive."

Warner producer Hal Wallis (who would later produce some of Davis' greatest films) concurred: "...there were moments when you weren't looking at Arliss, you were looking at her instead. There was no question in my mind that she would go all the way to the top." Jack Warner, too, liked what he saw and he signed Bette to a contract that would eventually stretch into eighteen turbulent years.

LEFT: Bette savors her newly-acquired status with fellow Warner contractee Ginger Rogers at the Coconut Grove nightclub in Hollywood. Her secure position at Warner allowed Davis to rent a new home, large enough to accommodate herself, Ruthie and Bobby. She also indulged herself with an expensive Auburn roadster that almost proved fatal to Bette when it burst into flame near the house. Quick-thinking Bobby pulled her sister to safety without a moment to spare, marking the first of a number of catastrophies and illnesses that would plague Davis during her life – making her enduring fame even more hard-earned than the public often realized.

BOTTOM LEFT: The Edna Ferber classic *So Big* began Bette's apprenticeship at Warner. She played a sensitive young artist in love with George Brent (pictured) and appeared in a brief scene with the picture's star, Barbara Stanwyck. The New York *Times* called Bette's performance "unusually competent."

OPPOSITE: Bette's resemblance to Constance Bennett is pronounced in this pose from *The Rich Are Always With Us*, a vehicle for Ruth Chatterton, then known as "The First Lady of The Screen." Again Davis played George Brent's love interest; this was now a bit of type casting since she had developed a crush on the handsome actor. Bette filmed her scenes in *The Rich Are Always With Us* concurrently with her work in *So Big*. She became accustomed to the rapid pace of film production, and had no less than *nine* pictures in release in 1932!

TOP RIGHT: In *The Dark Horse*, Davis played a political activist who ends up in the clinches of campaign manager Warren William. Bette's performance in this satirical comedy was hailed as "splendid" by the New York *Times*.

She embarked on a short publicity tour for the film, something which she found stressful: "I was always afraid people would say, 'Who is she?' Personal appearances always gave me the fear that the audience is going to be terrifically disappointed in me when compared with what they see on the screen."

CENTER RIGHT: Davis made her strongest impression on 1932 moviegoers in *Cabin in the Cotton*, playing the first of many "she-devil" roles, and vamping costar Richard Barthelmess (pictured). She did not enjoy working with director Michael Curtiz: "I would start a scene and Curtiz would mutter behind the camera, so that I could hear, 'God-damned-nothing-no-good-sexless-son-of-a-bitch!'—which might have little taste and less syntax, but a great deal of lucidity. What with Barthelmess's wife sitting beside the director appraising our love scenes and Curtiz heckling, it is a wonder I made it." Despite all this, Bette won many new fans as she cavorted sexily and uttered such dialogue as the immortal, "Ah'd love to kiss ya, but ah just washed mah hair." This was Davis' first attempt at playing an overtly sexual character and, the dialogue notwithstanding, she succeeded nicely. The New York *Herald Tribune* said, "Miss Davis shows a surprising vivacity as the seductive rich girl."

BOTTOM RIGHT: Harmon "Ham" Nelson and Bette pose following their surprise wedding in Yuma, Arizona, on August 18, 1932. The sudden decision to elope was Bette's, who admitted later that she felt she needed a familiar "anchor" to offset the often surreal aspects of her growing Hollywood fame. She saw in Nelson, "...home, New England, stability. I had been homesick for the world I had been brought up in."

The newlyweds spent their honeymoon travelling cross-country as part of a promotional tour for Warner's new musical, *Forty Second Street*. When they returned to the west coast they settled into a large new home with Ruthie and Bobby. Ham—who had come to Los An-

geles that summer to play trumpet in the Olympic Games ceremonies — soon formed his own band and found work in several popular nightclubs.

ABOVE: Ann Dvorak, Joan Blondell and Bette played former school chums who get together and recount their adventures in *Three On A Match*, Davis' final release of 1932 and a film she later called "a dull 'B' picture." Bette and Joan really had studied together at the Anderson-Milton School in New York, and the two actresses remained great friends for over fifty years until Blondell's death in 1979.

OPPOSITE: Davis and Blondell pose girlishly on the Santa Monica beach for publicity photos. This is one of the few times that Bette agreed to anything even approximating the "cheesecake" art so popular with studio photographers. "My legs have nothing to do with my talent," she once declared.

LEFT: Bette consoles her man—doomed mobster Spencer Tracy—in the prison melodrama *20,000 Years in Sing Sing*. Tracy was on "loan-out" from MGM for this film, and unfortunately this was the only time he worked with Davis, who once called him "one of my few acting idols." *20,000 Years in Sing Sing* was praised for its gritty portrayal of prison life, and it began a cycle of similar films produced at Warner all through the Thirties.

BELOW: A dramatic moment from Bette's next, *Parachute Jumper,* with Douglas Fairbanks, Jr., and Frank McHugh. Davis played, in her words, "a typist/moll" with the unlikely name of Alabama. The film was not a box-office winner.

23

BELOW: *The Working Man* reunited Bette with her mentor George Arliss (with Theodore Newton, left) in a comedy-drama about an unorthodox business executive who takes a job in his own factory to keep abreast of his workers. Davis played a frivolous girl who "straightens out" as a result of her exposure to Arliss.

Although Bette was now considered a star, she was still open to ad-

vice from the venerable Arliss; she wrote in her autobiography, "He taught me always to think of what came before a scene and what was to come after. Scenes being shot out of sequence are the devil to play."

LEFT: This portrait illustrates one of the several different "looks" the Warner makeup department tried on Bette during the first few years of her contract.

OPPOSITE: A magazine ad for *Ex-Lady* in which Bette is referred to as "filmdom's newest favorite." If that was a bit of an overstatement, it was indeed true that the versatility Davis had shown within the confines of her last few films had intrigued the public, and her popularity was growing steadily. She received over-the-title billing for the first time with this film.

25

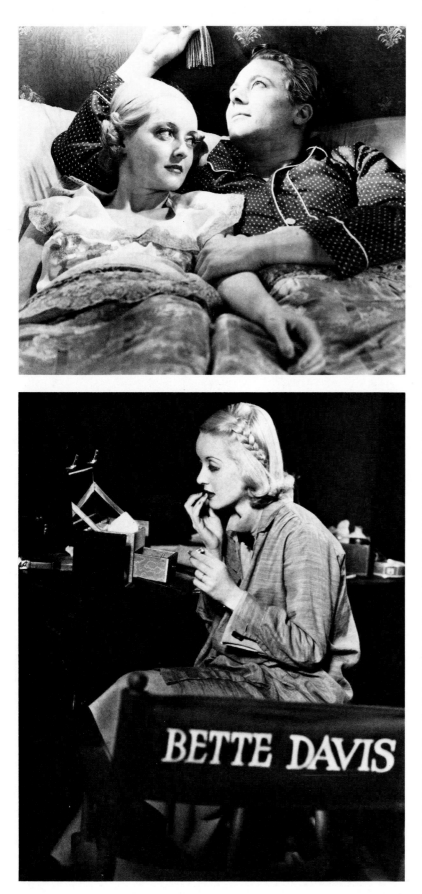

LEFT: Unfortunately, *Ex-Lady* was not an ideal star vehicle. Its supposedly "daring" storyline presented Bette as a glamorous commercial artist who feels that marriage is obsolete and convinces her lover (Gene Raymond, pictured) to live "in sin." Naturally, after a series of misunderstandings, Davis' character realizes the error of her ways and agrees to marry Raymond.

The picture was not a hit and Bette does not recall it with fondness. "I was made over and cast as the star of a piece of junk called *Ex-Lady*, which was supposed to be provocative—and provoked anyone of sensibility to nausea." Warner was disappointed with the public's reaction to both the film and Bette, so the studio returned her to formula films with strong male leads.

OPPOSITE: *Bureau Of Missing Persons* paired Davis with Pat O'Brien again and proved to be a snappy comedy-drama that made money. It was, however, a far cry from the film that Bette wanted very badly at the time to appear in—John Ford's production of *Mary of Scotland*, being prepared at RKO with Katharine Hepburn in the title role. Davis had long been fascinated with Queen Elizabeth I, read voraciously about her, and felt that she would be ideal in the part—especially opposite Hepburn, whom Bette greatly admired. Ford, however, was not impressed with Davis, and he cast Florence Eldridge in the role. Six years later, of course, Bette would have the last laugh by creating an unforgettable portrait of Elizabeth on screen in a film that would prove much more successful than Ford's.

BOTTOM LEFT: Warner gave Bette the full glamour treatment in *Fashions of 1934*, a fanciful look at *haute couture* that climaxes with elaborate Busby Berkeley musical numbers. *Photoplay* said the film was "packed with cleverness, spectacle, beauty, sophistication and tickling humor."

Davis was pleased to work opposite co-star William Powell, but she objected to this latest image the studio had devised for her. "I was glamorized beyond recognition... made to wear a platinum wig...to say nothing of the false eyelashes and the huge mouth." Despite her protests, Bette retained this appearance for her next few films.

RIGHT: Silent-screen heartthrob Charles Farrell in an intimate moment with Bette in *The Big Shakedown*, released in February 1934. The movie was a farfetched mixture of melodrama (Davis barely survives childbirth, but loses the baby) and gangland nastiness (a racketeer dies in a vat of acid). It was only a moderate success.

It was around this time that Bette was approached about portraying Mildred in *Of Human Bondage*, which was to begin production later in the year at RKO. Director John Cromwell had been impressed with Davis' work in *Cabin in the Cotton*, and he felt she would be ideal in the provocative W. Somerset Maugham character study. Bette couldn't have agreed more, but it took her almost six months of badgering to convince Jack Warner to acquiesce to this most important of loan-outs. In the meantime, Davis had four pictures on the home lot to get through.

BELOW: Bette and James Cagney are paired for the first time as a romantically involved boss and secretary in *Jimmy The Gent*, a typical Warner comedy directed at a break-neck pace by Michael Curtiz. *Variety* said of the picture, "Fans that want entertainment and don't care much about cinematic art will like this one." Sure enough, the picture was a popular success, but it took the studio seven years to come up with a suitable vehicle to reunite Cagney and Davis.

OPPOSITE: As a slumming society girl, Bette is strong-armed by Irving Pichel as an underworld nightclub czar in this moment from *Fog Over Frisco*. The film was a—by now—familiar mix of gangsters and the upper crust. According to *Variety*, Davis gave a "moderately good performance."

Two portraits from this period serve as proof that, in spite of her self-doubts, Bette Davis could hold her own against any of the most celebrated Hollywood beauties. The study on the right seems to have been inspired by the dramatic shots MGM circulated of Bette's friend Jean Harlow.

In 1982, Davis told Johnny Carson's television audience that during her youth she had always hated her face on the screen, but that with the perspective of fifty years she would sometimes watch her old films and think that she was "...the most gorgeous creature in the world... and sexy too!"

OPPOSITE: Another physical characteristic Davis was sensitive about was her neck, which she considered too long. However, in poses such as this, her neckline adds grace and elegance—and is one of the reasons she was able to wear often extreme fashions with aplomb.

ABOVE: Bette's next, *Housewife*, concerned a love triangle set against a background of radio advertising. Davis—seen here with John Halliday—lures George Brent away from Ann Dvorak, as the title character, only to lose him by film's end. Increasingly frustrated with the properties she was getting from the studio (she called *Housewife* a "horror"), Bette continued to beg the Warner brass to let her do *Of Human Bondage*.

RIGHT: Paul Muni warily offers Bette a light in this scene from *Bordertown*, a melodrama that offered Davis her best role in over a year. She played an unstable, sexually-deprived woman who murders her fat, older husband in order to seduce Muni, a Mexican would-be lawyer. Director Archie Mayo kept these lurid goings-on believable (in spite of Muni's hammy acting style), but he encountered obstinance from his leading lady.

In the film's final scenes, Bette was required to enact rapidly-advancing insanity as she tries to testify in a courtroom. Mayo wanted Davis to portray madness in an exaggerated "silent film" style. But she felt that a subtler approach would be more believable, and she went to the studio's front office fighting for her interpretation. Bette won her point, but only after agreeing to re-shoot the scene Mayo's way if audiences didn't understand her character's condition. Previews were held, and Davis' version succeeded beautifully. She had been proven right, but rather than winning the studio's admiration, she was instead labeled a meddling trouble maker.

OPPOSITE: The *Bordertown* costars are captured in a dramatic study by photographer Bert Longworth.

With the completion of *Housewife* and *Bordertown*, Bette was at last free to tackle *Of Human Bondage*. Worn down by her incessant pleading, Jack Warner finally agreed to a loan-out for the picture, but he was convinced that playing such an unremitting bitch as Mildred would prove disastrous for Bette's career. "Go hang yourself!" he told her. In order to make *Bondage*, Davis was forced to turn down another loan-out request. This one was from Frank Capra, who wanted Bette to play the runaway heiress in a comedy he was directing at Columbia titled *It Happened One Night*.

RIGHT: Leslie Howard as the sexually-obsessed medical student Phillip Carey and Bette as Mildred Rogers, the cruel, vulgar waitress who almost causes Phillip's ruination, pose during a break in the filming of *Of Human Bondage*. "The first few days on the set were not too heartwarming," Davis recalled in her autobiography. "Mr. Howard and his English colleagues were disturbed by the casting of an American girl in the part."

Anticipating this, Bette worked tirelessly to perfect Mildred's Cockney accent. She moved an English wardrobe woman into her home for two months in order to study her speech patterns and inflections. Practicing the accent day and night, Davis admitted that "I nearly drove my family mad. Poor Ham walked out of the house more than once and swore he'd never come back until I stopped talking like a Cockney."

OPPOSITE: Although he initially took a casual attitude toward the production (throwing Bette reaction lines for her closeups while he read a book off-stage), Leslie Howard soon realized that "the American girl" was stealing *Of Human Bondage* out from under his nose. Wisely, he began to take his participation (and Davis) more seriously. As a result, he brought subtle nuances to Phillip that helped audiences better understand why he put up with Mildred's obvious connivings.

Bette was completely exhausted as filming on *Bondage* ended, and although she felt pride in her performance, she held great doubts about how the public would respond to such a downbeat story with such an unlikable heroine. Her fears were not allayed when Ham told her that he admired the performance, but that it was so powerfully honest that he feared for its popularity. Davis steeled herself for a depressing "I told you so" from Jack Warner.

Happily, when *Of Human Bondage* opened in June 1934, it was to rapturous reviews and tremendous public reaction. Audiences *loved* hating Mildred, cheered when she is finally denounced by Phillip, and had no difficulty distinguishing between the hateful character on the screen and the gifted actress who brought her so vividly to life.

Overnight, Davis became the talk of the film industry and an Oscar nomination seemed a sure thing. RKO, however, made a crucial mistake by submitting Bette's performance in the Best Supporting category. As a result, she missed out on a nomination of any kind. "My failure to receive the award created a scandal that gave me more publicity than if I had won it," Davis said later. "...columnists spread the word 'foul' and the public stood behind me like an army." This was more than could be said of her home studio. Warner showed Bette token support by urging a write-in campaign for her performance on the Oscar ballot, but many factions at the studio considered her work in *Bondage* a fluke.

Davis was astonished that after giving what *Life* magazine called "probably the best performance ever recorded on the screen by a U.S. actress," she had gained so little respect from the studio that was supposedly grooming her for greatness. Even wonderful reviews for her work in *Bordertown* (filmed before, but released after, *Bondage*) didn't move Warner to upgrade Bette's position.

BELOW: Ex-showgirl-turned-land-lady Alison Skipworth offers advice to Bette as *The Girl From 10th Avenue*, the slight romantic comedy-drama Warner stuck Davis with fresh from her triumph in *Of Human Bondage*. The picture was a success, wholly because of Bette's ability and her growing appeal to the movie-going public.

OPPOSITE TOP: As rival reporters, George Brent and Bette pose against a backdrop of newspaper headlines in *Front Page Woman*. In this typical Thirties battle of the sexes, Bette solves a murder mystery in order to refute Brent's claim that "women make bum newspapermen."

Although Bette has never confirmed the gossip, it is generally agreed that by this time, she was deeply in love with George Brent and that they were engaged in a serious love affair that lasted for over a year.

OPPOSITE BOTTOM: With George Brent again in *Special Agent*, Bette was once more embroiled in the Warner specialty of gangsters and racketeering. The New York *Times* called the picture "a machine-gun saga" and joined with other periodicals in pondering why the studio wasn't making better use of Davis' talents.

LEFT: Bette, Ham and vocalist Eadie Adams are photographed at the piano of the Cinegrill nightclub in the Hollywood Roosevelt Hotel. Ham fronted the club's band and achieved a local celebrity status, but it in no way rivaled his wife's fame. This disparity in the Nelsons' careers led to a great deal of friction. Bette admitted years later that she had submitted to an abortion in 1933 because she knew that Ham would be miserable as a father who was not the chief breadwinner of the family. She reflected, "I was filled with compassion that was streaked with irritation. I wanted to stay married, but our reversed roles debilitated him . . . and drove me to distraction."

Davis was also distracted around this time by an unexpected visit from her father, who was in Los Angeles on business. After an awkward dinner at Bette's home, he patronizingly told her, "Your husband is a nice young boy." Less than a year later, Harlow Davis died, having never told his daughter that he was proud of her accomplishments.

BOTTOM LEFT: Bette with her *Dangerous* costar Franchot Tone, whom she described as "lovely to play with." Interestingly, rumors persist that the two stars engaged in a love affair during the production of this film, and that Tone's wife at the time, Joan Crawford, considered Davis a serious rival for her husband's affections.

OPPOSITE: As troubled actress Joyce Heath, Bette is contemplative in this scene from *Dangerous*, the film that brought her the first of two Oscars, in spite of a script Davis considered "maudlin and mawkish." She worked "like ten men" to bring to life this story of a self-destructive young woman (loosely based on the life of stage star Jeanne Eagles) who finds salvation only after she has crippled her husband in an intentional automobile accident.

OPPOSITE: *Dangerous* may not have been an ideal vehicle for Bette, but it was the best showcase Warner had offered since *Bordertown*, and she made the most of it. Her reviews were excellent, and included E. Arnot Robertson's famous remarks for *Picture Post*: "I think Bette Davis would probably have been burned as a witch if she had lived two or three hundred years ago. She gives the curious feeling of being charged with a power which can find no ordinary outlet." The New York *Times* called her performance "strikingly sensitive."

RIGHT: Bette holds the Oscar she received as the Best Actress of 1935 in *Dangerous*, as Victor McLaglen looks on. Davis later confided that the excitement of the evening (her victory was announced by film pioneer D.W. Griffith) was blunted by the realization that she considered the honor a "consolation prize" for her work in *Of Human Bondage*, and that she believed the best performance by an actress in 1935 to be Katharine Hepburn's in *Alice Adams*.

The plain dress Davis chose to wear to the Oscar dinner drew criticism from the press—and from Ruthie, who told her, "You are a star, Bette, a great star and people look to you to be well groomed." Although she was a frequent visitor to Bette's movie sets, Ruthie was careful not to offer advice or criticize her daughter's work. She was, however, always concerned about appearances, and tried to encourage Bette to dress more glamorously off screen.

It was at this time that Bette took credit for naming the Academy trophy Oscar. She claims that the statue's backside reminded her of Ham's, and she came up with Oscar because it was his middle name. Several others have sworn *they* named the trophy, and to this day, the Academy has remained diplomatically non-committal about the origin of its representative's name.

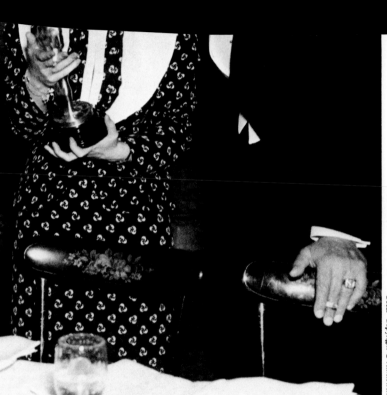

"Oscar" Copyright © A.M.P.A.S.

OPPOSITE TOP: This 1935 portrait indicates that the studio makeup department was beginning to realize that Bette's natural, unique looks didn't require major cosmetic overhauling. For character roles, of course, Davis has always been fearless about altering her appearance for the requirements of a role—no matter how unflattering the results might be.

OPPOSITE BOTTOM: Leslie Howard, Dick Foran, Bette and Humphrey Bogart in a tense moment from *The Petrified Forest*, based on Robert E. Sherwood's successful stage play. The often-imitated plot concerns a group of disparate characters thrown together in an Arizona roadhouse and held captive by a gang of hoodlums on the lam. The script was a carefully-constructed psychological study that served all of the actors well, but especially Bogart as gangster Duke Mantee. His performance in this film assured his future as a screen legend.

RIGHT: Davis played Gabby, a restless girl who waits tables in the cafe, but yearns to study art in Paris. She falls in love with Howard as Alan Squier, an idealistic drifter who encourages Gabby's dreams. Their brief liaison ends tragically when Alan is shot and killed by Mantee.

The Petrified Forest was a substantial success with both the public and film critics. The New York *Times* wrote, "...there should be a large measure of praise for Bette Davis, who demonstrates that she does not have to be hysterical to be credited with a grand portrayal." Bette enjoyed this second association with Howard, telling a reporter, "This time he was delighted to work with me and absolutely charming. Leslie had by now become so warm and chummy that throughout one scene where we lay on the floor, victimized by Bogie, he kept nibbling on my arm."

OPPOSITE: An unusual publicity photo from Bette's second 1936 release, *The Golden Arrow*, in which she played a cafeteria cashier masquerading as a madcap heiress—a breed of screen heroine the public was rapidly tiring of. Although the New York *Times* called Davis' performance "saucy," this frothy comedy (her sixth picture with George Brent) did nothing to advance her career. She told Whitney Stine, "I was actually insulted to have to appear in such a cheap, nothing story after *Of Human Bondage*, *The Petrified Forest* and *Bordertown*."

ABOVE: Bette was even more disappointed in her next picture, *Satan Met A Lady*, a muddled version of Dashiell Hammett's classic *The Maltese Falcon*, costarring Warren William (seen here). The film was called "disconnected and lunatic" by critic Bosley Crowther, who proposed a "Bette Davis Reclamation Project" to "prevent the waste of this gifted lady's talents."

But Davis didn't need Crowther to remind her that her career was once again in the doldrums. When the studio announced that she would next be cast as a female lumberjack (!) in a script titled *God's Country and the Woman*, she finally rebelled and went on suspension, telling the press, "If I continue to appear in mediocre pictures, I'll have no career worth fighting for."

In an attempt to get Davis to accept *God's Country*, Jack Warner told her that he was optioning a new novel about the old South, *Gone With The Wind*, with a lead that would be ideal for her. "Yes," responded Davis, "and I'll just bet it's a dilly!"

After several weeks of failed negotiations with the studio, Bette accepted an offer from a British producer to film two pictures; one in England and the second in France opposite Maurice Chevalier. Most importantly, Davis was guaranteed script approval on both. Within a short time, she and Ham were sailing to England, incorporating a second honeymoon into this risky career gamble. Meanwhile, back in Hollywood, Warner was considering legal action against its wayward star.

LEFT: October 1936. Bette in London on her way to court, where her suspension dispute with Warner Brothers had ended up. By leaving America, Davis believed that she had avoided any legal moves from the studio, but in September Warner filed an injunction, through the British system, to prevent Bette from appearing in films produced by any other company.

The court battle was acrimonious; the studio lawyers depicted Davis as a "naughty girl" who was spoiled, greedy (although she had never demanded more money) and ungrateful, while Bette's counsel stressed artistic enslavement and the studio's seeming sabotage of an important career. After several days of testimony, the court decided in Warner Brothers' favor, and Bette was requested to return to Hollywood to honor her contract.

Even though she had lost the case, she took consolation in knowing that she had at least shown other contract actors that the studios *could* be challenged. Prior to leaving England, Bette enjoyed a warm reunion with George Arliss, who advised her, "Go back... you haven't lost as much as you think. Go back and accept the decision."

BOTTOM LEFT: A bearded Bette attends a costume party with Ham, who is dressed as a hobo. When the Nelsons returned to America, Ham decided to remain in New York for a while in order to advance his career within the booming "Big Band" industry. A fine musician, Nelson eventually recorded with several top orchestras (including Tommy Dorsey's), but he was never able to attain stardom during the "swing" era. His chief claim to fame remained his marriage to Bette.

Davis encouraged Ham's musical aspirations in the hope that any success he attained would soften his growing resentment toward her. Nelson's personality had changed since his marriage to Bette. He had become bitter and jealous, often lashing out at her in front of friends, and whining to her in private. Bette was slowly losing respect for him.

ABOVE: A stiffly-posed behind-the-scenes look at Bette in costume for *Marked Woman*, her first film at Warner following the legal battle. She is a nightclub hostess (a Thirties euphemism for prostitute), who lies in court to protect her gangster boss. But after he has her severely beaten, she decides to testify against him with the encouragement of special prosecutor Humphrey Bogart.

The film was not a masterpiece, but it was certainly superior to Bette's last few vehicles, and she considered it a "good picture." Most critics agreed, citing its timeliness; "culled right from the front-page headlines, a tabloid story come true," said the New York *Sun*. Bette, too, received excellent notices. *Variety* offered the supreme actor's compliment: "She is among the Hollywood few who can submerge themselves in a role to the point where they become the character they are playing."

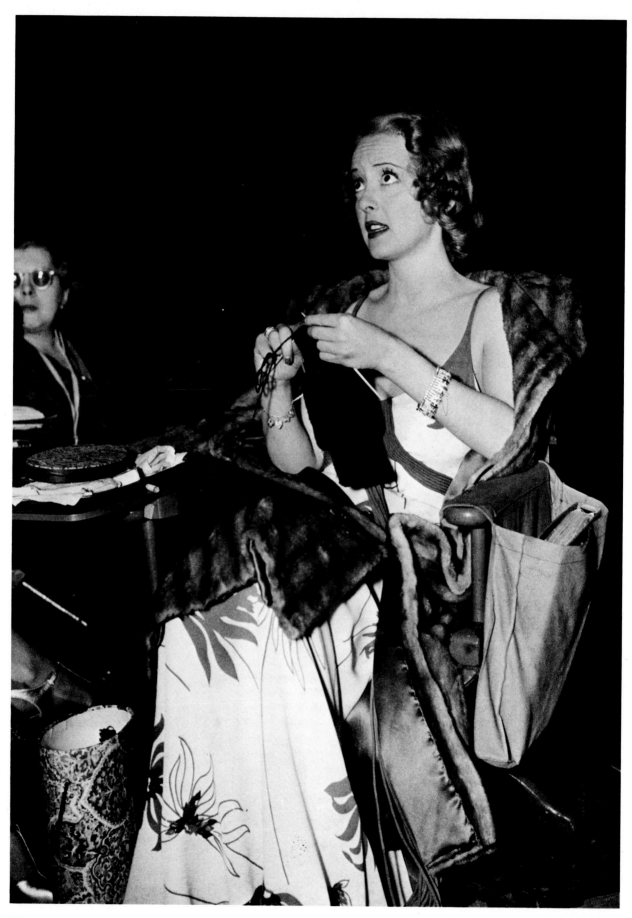

RIGHT: Customarily during the Thirties and Forties, popular films were recreated on radio with as many of the original cast members as possible. Here, *Marked Woman* is presented in an abbreviated version on Louella Parson's weekly show; left to right are Humphrey Bogart, Parsons, Bette, Jane Bryan and Eduardo Cianelli. Davis enjoyed appearing on the radio; she was never snobbish about where she worked. It was an attitude that would serve her well when television became a major entertainment force fifteen years later.

OPPOSITE: Between scenes on *Kid Galahad*, Davis indulges in her favorite on-set pastime, knitting. Her role as Edward G. Robinson's mistress in this film (still considered

one of the best boxing movies ever made) was peripheral to the plot, but she took it to reach an audience that might not otherwise see her. She explained at the time, "*Kid Galahad*, while not giving me much of a role in the artistic sense, has such a lot of good robust fight stuff in it that it is bound to appeal to a totally different audience...with which I nevertheless need to be kept in touch."

LEFT: On a tricycle, Davis poses with her movie son Jackie Day on the set of *That Certain Woman*, the melodrama that served as Bette's first foray into the genre of "women's pictures" so popular at the time. Under the direction of Edmund Goulding, Davis delivered a multi-leveled performance as a young woman who suffers through widowhood at seventeen, then marries Henry Fonda, becomes pregnant as a result of their one and only night together and is eventually forced to give up her son. Bette admitted that the plot "tasted a bit of soap," but critics applauded the commitment she brought to her role, and the film was a box-office success.

RIGHT: Between scenes of *That Certain Woman*, Fonda seems to have fallen asleep in mid-conversation, much to Bette's annoyance. This may have been a gag shot, posed for the benefit of an on-set photographer. Davis and Fonda enjoyed an easy rapport off screen, and although this was their first film appearance together, they had known each other for years; their paths had crossed several times a decade before when they were both involved in summer stock productions in New England, and Fonda always claimed to have given Bette one of her first kisses while she was still a student at the Cushing Academy.

BOTTOM RIGHT: The final Davis release of 1937 was *It's Love I'm After*, a breezy comedy that brought Bette and Leslie Howard together again, this time as bickering, married stage stars in the style of Noel Coward. It was a welcome change of pace for both actors (and costar Olivia de Havilland), and it delighted the critics. The New York *Times* called it "a rippling farce, brightly written and deftly directed." The picture was another hit with the public.

Bette looks adoringly at Ham as they attend a symphony concert in Los Angeles. How the Nelson marriage was going at any given time depended often on what was happening with the Davis career. Her husband had to be prepared for a variety of moods from Bette, who once said, "It is small wonder that Ham was both dazzled, bewitched and then exhausted with my crises. I always had one."

After making three movies in five months, Davis was exhausted following *It's Love I'm After*, and she wanted nothing more than a brief vacation while Warner prepared what she hoped would be her next vehicle—*Jezebel*, based on a short-lived Broadway play that she had been urging the studio to acquire for her for some time. Jack Warner, however, wanted her to rush immediately into *Hollywood Hotel*, a formula comedy in which she would play in support of crooner Dick Powell. Davis risked another suspension by flatly refusing to work in the film, and after much heated correspondence between studio and star, the matter was dropped and Bette was allowed an extensive rest.

OPPOSITE: Davis is serene and confident in this pose taken just prior to her ascent to superstardom. After proving her versatility and professionalism in thirty-five films in less than seven years, Bette felt that she had earned the right to limit the number of pictures she made each year, and to hold out for scripts of only exceptional quality. Thanks to the box-office success of her last few films, and in spite of their recent disagreements, Warner surprisingly agreed—and began working closely with Bette to enable her to become Hollywood's premiere dramatic star. To her delight, *Jezebel* was now ready to help Davis achieve this goal.

TOP LEFT: In costume for *Jezebel*, Bette takes a call on the set—and her animated expression is indicative of the excitement she was feeling as this production got underway. As every film historian knows, it is impossible to discuss *Jezebel* without more than one reference to *Gone With The Wind*.

In the two years since Davis had pooh-poohed Jack Warner when he suggested she would be perfect in the lead of a southern story he was negotiating for, *Gone With The Wind* had not only become a publishing phenomenon, but with the sale of the film rights, it was also the hottest topic of Hollywood speculation as well. Warner had acquired the rights, but sold them to David O. Selznick—who immediately instigated the greatest publicity ploy in film history: the search for an actress ideally suited to play Scarlett O'Hara.

Bette was the star most often suggested for the role in polls taken in the movie fan magazines, and at one point Selznick definitely wanted her —but only on Jack Warner's condition that she work opposite Errol Flynn as Rhett Butler. Knowing Flynn lacked the acting prowess to do justice to the Butler role, and that his miscasting would adversely affect her performance, Davis had to decline Selznick's offer. Thanks to *Jezebel*, however, Bette was given the opportunity to play a Scarlett-like character in a beautifully-produced film that played successfully to movie audiences a full year before *Gone With The Wind* premiered.

BOTTOM LEFT: As Julie in *Jezebel*, Bette is comforted by her aunt

(Continued on next page)

(played by Fay Bainter). Julie is a self-centered, temperamental New Orleans debutante who loses her fiance, Pres (Henry Fonda), after humiliating him in public, tries in vain to win him back after he has married, and then tricks another suitor, Buck (played by George Brent), into a duel with Pres that results in Buck's death. At the end of the film Julie seeks redemption by nursing Pres through a fever epidemic, promising to return him to his wife when he is cured.

A story this melodramatic could have been unbelievable on the screen, but fortunately producer Hal Wallis hired William Wyler to direct, and he gave the picture a sensibility and a stature that a lesser artist might not have achieved. Wyler also drew a wondrous performance from Davis, one which brought raves from the critics. The *National Board of Review* said, "Her Julie is the peak of her accomplishments, so far, and what is ahead is unpredictable, depending on her luck and on the wisdom of her producers." Bette's performance earned her an Oscar nomination; Fay Bainter was also nominated for her supporting role, as was the film in the Best Picture category.

RIGHT: Fonda and Davis pose for a romantic publicity portrait on the *Jezebel* set. Bette was delighted to be working opposite Fonda again, but his personal life intruded on the shooting schedule when he had to return to the east coast before filming was completed in order to be with his wife as she awaited the birth of their daughter Jane. Davis had to deliver some of her most difficult closeup scenes without Fonda to play against. In 1977, Jane Fonda hosted the American Film Institute's Life Achievement salute to Davis, and she took the opportunity to publicly apologize for her father's absence during the final days of *Jezebel* filming.

BELOW: Bette and Ham are photographed at the Coconut Grove nightclub. As usual, Davis is the center of attention as she carries on an enthusiastic conversation. In contrast, her husband seems ill-at-ease and pensive. At this point, the Nelson marriage was floundering badly;

both stars' names are placed above the title.

OPPOSITE: A lovely study of Bette in *The Sisters*, taken by Warner photographer Schuyler Crail. Before starting the film, Davis went on another brief suspension from the studio to avoid what she considered two inferior projects, *Comet Over Broadway*, about an actress whose husband is an ex-con, and a Busby Berkeley-directed musical, *Garden of the Moon*, that was eventually filmed with Margaret Lindsay in the role planned for Bette.

It was dismaying for Davis that after winning an Oscar, and bringing glory to the studio as its leading female star, she "...was asked to appear again in junk." One project that both she and Warner agreed upon was *The Miracle*, in which Bette would have played a nun under the direction of Max Reinhardt. Although technicolor tests were filmed of Davis in costume, the production never got off the ground because of script problems and legal difficulties.

Ham was more uncomfortable than ever in his position as Queen's consort, and Bette grew more and more resentful about being the family moneymaker. Their relationship was deteriorating rapidly, and there was now very little communication between them. Added to this situation was the badly-kept secret that Bette had fallen in love with William Wyler during *Jezebel* production.

RIGHT: Davis cuddles with heartthrob Errol Flynn in *The Sisters*, her final 1938 film. Originally intended as a vehicle for soap-opera queen Kay Francis, the story called for Bette to marry the dashing but irresponsible Flynn, suffer through his abandonment, a miscarriage, and the 1906 San Francisco earthquake. In the end she and the apologetic Flynn are reunited happily. As acted by Davis and directed by Anatole Litvak, *The Sisters* proved to be an engrossing and popular melodrama that served to heighten Bette's stature with the public.

Although she was initially excited about working with Errol Flynn, Davis soon came to resent him for his cavalier approach to his work and also because the studio gave him top billing. Originally, Flynn was to receive sole billing over the title, until Bette protested. In the final ads,

TOP RIGHT: September 1938: Howard Hughes buys a raffle ticket from Bette at The Tailwaggers Party, a benefit to aid animals. In his book *Bette*, Charles Higham details an intense—though relatively brief—affair between Hughes and Davis. Hughes was involved at the time in an on-again off-again romance with Katharine Hepburn, and it seems that he was attracted to Davis because he found her less beautiful than Hepburn and consequently less of a threat to his reportedly fragile ego where women were concerned. The liaison turned bizarre when Ham tape-recorded the lovers in action and blackmailed Hughes for seventy-thousand dollars. Reportedly, a mortified Bette repaid the entire amount to Hughes over an extended period. Needless to say, the episode ended the Nelson marriage as well as the romance with Hughes.

As Davis was nearing the peak of her career, her personal life was in shambles. Following the collapse of her marriage, she suffered further heartache when William Wyler (whom she still cared deeply for) suddenly married another actress. Wyler reportedly adored Bette for her talent and down-to-earth personality, but he also considered her to be obsessive and "neurotic." He had recently been divorced from a gifted actress, Margaret Sullavan, who shared similar qualities, and he was not prepared to repeat a painful experience. A brief fling with her *Sisters* director Anatole Litvak brought Bette little comfort, and she found herself, at thirty-one, more emotionally dependent on Ruthie than she had been since they had left the east coast.

BOTTOM RIGHT: Spencer Tracy and Bette pose happily with their Academy Awards after being named the Best Actor and Actress of 1938. Davis was especially delighted to have won the award for her work in *Jezebel*, as she was confident that it was voted to her on the basis of merit, and not as a consolation prize —as she felt her first Oscar had been. Also from *Jezebel*, Fay Bainter was chosen as the year's Best Supporting Actress.

ABOVE: Conrad Nagel—the star of Bette's first film *Bad Sister*—visits her and costar Humphrey Bogart on the set of *Dark Victory*, the first of four outstanding Davis releases in 1939.

Originating as a stage vehicle for Tallulah Bankhead, *Dark Victory* afforded Davis an acting field day as the terminally ill society girl Judith Traherne, who initially reacts to the news of her condition by frantically "living it up" until she finds contentment in her final months by marrying her sensitive doctor, played by reliable George Brent.

Bette's touching performance, free of mawkish sentimentality, was sup-ported beautifully by a strong cast that included (besides Bogart and Brent) Geraldine Fitzgerald and Ronald Reagan. Davis has special words for Bogart's contribution. "I thought his performance (as a sympathetic stable hand) was just perfect. We had some very difficult scenes to play. . .I thanked God for the help his performance gave me in playing mine."

OPPOSITE: A dramatic portrait of Bette in *Dark Victory*, complete with what had become her personal trademark and favorite acting prop: a cigarette. Bette's work in this film remains one of her most popular performances, and after forty-five years it holds up remarkably well. Critics of the day were highly impressed—even though brilliant Davis performances were becoming commonplace. The New York *Times* raved, "Miss Davis is superb. More than that, she is enchanted and enchanting. Admittedly it is a great role—rangy, full-bodied, designed for a virtuosa, almost sure to invite the faint damning of 'tour de force.' But that must not detract from the eloquence, the tenderness, the heartbreaking sincerity with which she played it." Bette was again Oscar-nominated for this role, and *Dark Victory* received a nomination for Best Picture.

TOP RIGHT: For the historical drama *Juarez*, Davis adopted an exotic appearance to play Carlotta, the mentally-unbalanced wife of Maximilian (played by Brian Aherne), the newly-appointed Emperor of Mexico in the 1860s. Conceived as a showcase for top-billed Paul Muni in the title role of the revered Mexican President, *Juarez* offered Bette a distinct change of pace as a woman who is emotionally unprepared for the turbulent events that engulf her family and lead eventually to her husband's execution.

BOTTOM RIGHT: Bette won critical acclaim for her final scenes in *Juarez*, when she has to convey Carlotta's descent from mental confusion to utter madness as she realizes that neither her fervent prayers nor her pleading with Napoleon III (Claude Rains) will save her doomed husband.

In her autobiography, Davis admitted to being intimidated by Rains. "...he scared the life out of me. When he looked at me during our scene as Napoleon would look at Carlotta, with loathing, I thought he Claude Rains held loathing of me Bette Davis as a performer!" As it turned out, Rains was a great Davis fan, and the two actors went on to work together brilliantly in three more pictures.

OPPOSITE: *The Old Maid* brought Bette her first opportunity to play a character who matures from youth to old age. She is the naive-but-pregnant young bride waiting in vain for her groom (played by the everpresent George Brent), who has been killed in the Civil War. We then see her (below) as the sixty-year-old spinster who has sacrificed her life for the sake of her illegitimate daughter.

BELOW RIGHT: Davis with Cecilia Loftus and Miriam Hopkins, her costars in *The Old Maid*. There was considerable tension during the production of this film, thanks to Hopkins' determination to undermine Bette's performance. Hopkins had known Davis since the days of the Cukor stock company, and although she too had achieved stardom, she was irrationally jealous of Bette's standing in the film community. During the first few days of production on *The Old Maid*, Hopkins appeared on the set wearing a gown that was an exact duplicate of one Davis had worn in *Jezebel*. (Hopkins had starred in *Jezebel* on Broadway.)

The anticipated blow-up between the two actresses never happened, however, because, as Bette told Whitney Stine, "To Miriam's utter disappointment I gave no indication I had any idea that her costume was a copy of mine..." Hopkins' attempts to sabotage Davis' work failed, and the picture was well received by the public and the press. Bette had proven to her studio that she was ready to realize her long-standing dream of portraying England's aging Queen Elizabeth I.

LEFT: Bette's final—and most daring —1939 performance was in *The Private Lives of Elizabeth and Essex*, opposite Errol Flynn. Based on Maxwell Anderson's acclaimed verse-play *Elizabeth The Queen*, this project presented Davis with her greatest acting challenge to date: playing the unlovely English monarch (thirty-five years her senior), who places her country in peril because of her passionate love for the much-younger Earl of Essex (Flynn). As thrilled as Davis was with the role, she was not pleased with the casting of Flynn. She said later, "I used to dream that Laurence Olivier was Essex."

BELOW: As no other female star of her era had done, Bette allowed her good looks to be completely obscured for her role as Elizabeth I. She insisted that Perc Westmore and his staff shave off her eyebrows and several inches of her hairline for the sake of authenticity. She felt courageous about the decision because of advice she had taken from Charles Laughton, who once told her, "Never stop daring to hang yourself, Bette!"

OPPOSITE: In the midst of *Elizabeth and Essex* filming, Davis sat for this unflattering "glamour" portrait that couldn't disguise the false eyelashes, drawn-on eyebrows and wig that her role as Queen Elizabeth necessitated. Fortunately, the sacrifice of Bette's beauty paid off in surprisingly strong box office and good reviews for the picture. The New York *Times* said, "Bette Davis' Elizabeth is a strong, resolute, glamour-skimping characterization against which Mr. Flynn's Essex has about as much chance as a beanshooter against a tank."

ABOVE: Following completion of *The Private Lives of Elizabeth and Essex*, Ruthie and Bette attend an art exhibit in Los Angeles. Davis was once again exhausted and had lost an alarming amount of weight. Before starting any new films, she was encouraged (for once) by Jack Warner to take a leave of absence to regain her strength. She chose to realize a lifelong ambition by taking a leisurely automobile tour of New England. In the process, she bought Butternut, a beautiful old home in the Sugar Hill section of New Hampshire. She also met, and slowly fell in love with, a handsome, rugged inn keeper named Arthur Farnsworth, who would become her second husband within a year's time.

OPPOSITE: Davis sat for this unusual portrait by Bert Six as her first decade as a film actress came to a close. Although it had taken longer than she had anticipated, she was now a star of the first magnitude: she had survived several "image" changes to emerge as Hollywood's most courageous dramatic actress.

The public was fascinated by her ability to submerge herself into a demanding character role while at the same time retaining unique personality traits that were the delight of nightclub mimics. Her distinctive walk, expressive eyes, clipped speech pattern and quirky way of puffing on a cigarette had become familiar mannerisms to filmgoers the world over. She had also earned the respect and affection of the press, who had recently dubbed her "Popeye The Magnificent" and "The Duse of the Depression Era." As the Thirties ended, Bette was finally secure in a well-earned position at the top of her profession.

THE
FORTIES

RIGHT: As Ed Sullivan looks on, Bette and Mickey Rooney congratulate each other as they are crowned 1940's King and Queen of the Movies as the result of a poll taken of over twenty-three million newspaper readers from across the United States. Davis was flattered by the honor, but it was just one of several titles being bandied about to describe her impact on the industry and the public. Some Hollywood wags were now calling her The Fourth Warner Brother, while in other circles she was already being hailed as the First Lady of the Screen.

OPPOSITE: Davis in her first 1940 film, *All This, And Heaven Too*, based on Rachel Field's novel about a real-life scandal in mid-nineteenth-century France. She played Henriette Desportes, a governess who was accused of carrying on an affair with her married employer, the Duc de Praslin, and then murdering his wife.

Initially, Bette was not interested in another period costume drama, but the role of the Governess offered her an opportunity to underplay and bring out subtleties in the character. Also, Davis became very friendly with author Field, and they spent many long visits discussing whether or not the Governess was indeed guilty of both the affair and the murder. Field believed firmly in Desportes' innocence, and had little trouble convincing Bette, who claimed that this belief added an extra dimension to her performance.

BOTTOM RIGHT: The casting of Charles Boyer as the Duc pleased Bette enormously. Calling him "... this romantic, beautiful actor," she credits him with bringing the undefined relationship between the governess and the Duc into sharp focus for the audience. Working again under the direction of Anatole Litvak, Davis gave a sensitive performance that earned her another Oscar nomination. *All This, and Heaven Too* was Warner's prestige release of the year, and although some critics found it sluggish at almost two-and-a-half hours in length, it received an Academy Award nomination as the Best Film of 1940.

TOP RIGHT: At ceremonies in Beverly Hills, Douglas Churchill, the motion picture editor of *Redbook* magazine, presents Davis with an elaborate trophy for "Advancing the Art of the Motion Picture." Offering congratulations are D.W. Griffith, left, and Merle Oberon. Bette was rapidly becoming the most honored actress in Hollywood; almost weekly she was topping popularity polls or receiving citations of merit from one group or another.

BOTTOM RIGHT: The dramatic opening moments of *The Letter*: Davis as Leslie Crosbie has just shot and killed her lover Geoffrey Hammond (David Newell). Later she convinces her husband, but not the local constable, that she killed Hammond in self-defense when he tried to molest her. Following a brief trial, Leslie is acquitted—but is soon murdered by Hammond's widow (Gale Sondegaard in a memorable performance).

The bare plot of *The Letter*, from a play by W. Somerset Maugham, does not convey the singular mood of the film as acted by the principals and directed by William Wyler. Cinematographer Tony Gaudio worked closely with Wyler to brilliantly exploit the story's locale, a Malaysian rubber plantation. The resulting camera angles and exotic lighting effects (not seen since the Von Sternberg/Dietrich films of the early Thirties) gave *The Letter* an atmosphere of mystery and intrigue.

OPPOSITE: Herbert Marshall, as Leslie's blindly devoted husband Robert, comforts his wife even after she has admitted that the trial was a farce, and that she murdered her lover—a longtime friend of Robert's—in cold blood. 1940 audiences were shocked when Bette, as Leslie, shouts passionately to her husband, "With all my heart, I still love the man I killed!"

RIGHT: Bette's performance in *The Letter* drew enthusiastic reviews. The New York *Times* said, "Miss Davis is a strangely cool and calculating killer who conducts herself with reserve and yet implies a deep confusion of emotions." *The Hollywood Reporter* offered, "Bette Davis has to divide honors of this great triumph with...William Wyler." Their past relationship notwithstanding, Davis and Wyler had several vocal, on-set disagreements that at one point resulted in Bette walking off the set for the first time in her career.

Fortunately, none of this strife was evident in the finished product, and *The Letter* was a terrific success, earning an Oscar nomination for Best Picture. Davis, too, was nominated for the third consecutive time in the Best Actress category. Following completion of *The Letter*, Davis returned to her new home in New England for a rest and a reunion with Arthur Farnsworth.

OPPOSITE: In late October 1940, Bette poses for a wardrobe test for her new film *The Great Lie*, which tells the soapish story of a glamorous concert pianist, played by Mary Astor, who impulsively marries a wealthy playboy (George Brent) and naturally becomes pregnant after their *one* night together before the marriage is annulled for legal reasons. Brent returns to his long-suffering ex-fianceé (Davis)and they are married, but he is shortly sent to South America, where his plane crashes and for some time he is presumed dead. In the meantime, Astor secretly gives birth to Brent's child, but agrees to give it up to Davis, who tells everyone (including the safely-returned Brent) that it is *her* baby. Eventually the truth comes out and Astor nobly allows Davis and Brent to raise her child as their own.

BOTTOM RIGHT: Davis was instrumental in the casting of Mary Astor in *The Great Lie*. She respected her as an actress and knew that Astor's talent as a pianist would add believability to her role. Just days into production, Davis (with the approval of director Edmund Goulding) elicited Astor's help in the rewriting of their scenes to bring more credibility to the script. In the process, Astor's part took on added shading which she conveyed beautifully in her performance. No one

was more thrilled than Bette when Astor won an Oscar for her supporting role. Following the ceremonies Davis sent her a telegram saying, "We did it!"

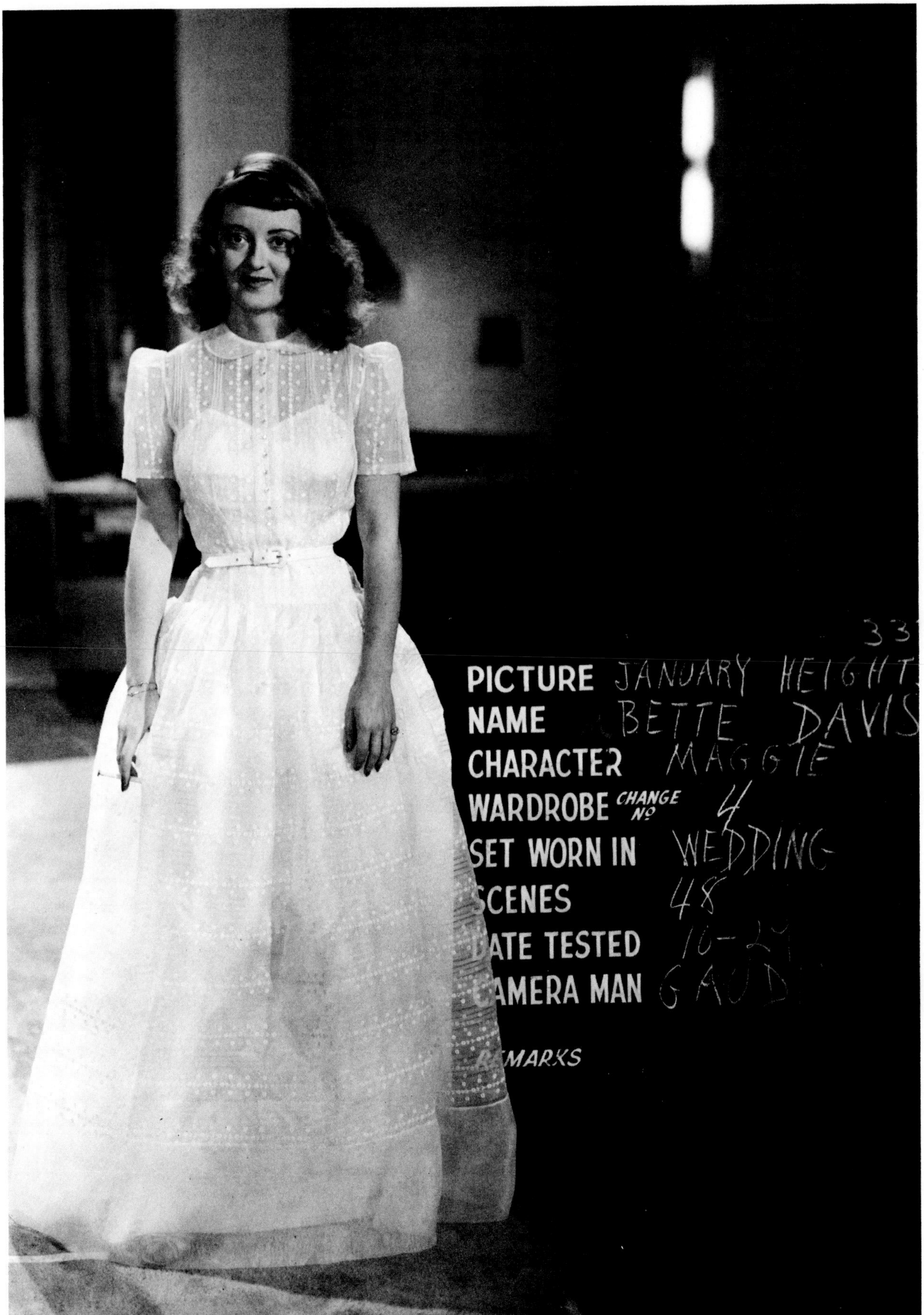

PICTURE JANUARY HEIGHT

NAME BETTE DAVIS

CHARACTER MAGGIE

WARDROBE *CHANGE NO* 4

SET WORN IN WEDDING

SCENES 48

DATE TESTED 10-2

CAMERA MAN GAUD

REMARKS

BELOW: Arthur Farnsworth and his bride cut the cake following their wedding on New Year's Eve, 1940, at a private ranch in Rimrock, Arizona. Bette had been remarkably successful in keeping her wedding plans a secret from both the studio and the press. She purposely married on a holiday so that half-staffed newspapers would be caught off-guard and she and "Farney" could enjoy their wedding in as much privacy as possible.

Unfortunately, Davis' schedule did not permit a lengthy honeymoon, so the newlyweds returned to her home, Riverbottom, in the Glendale section of Los Angeles. Less than two weeks later, Bette reported to Warner for the film that would reunite her with James Cagney.

OPPOSITE: Fans of both Davis and Cagney had been writing to the studio requesting a change from the heavy dramatics the two stars had been specializing in for their past several pictures. *The Bride Came C.O.D.* was the result. The script presented a shopworn comic premise: a madcap heiress (Davis) betrothed to a slick band leader (Jack Carson) is thrown into an implausible situation with a rough-edged maverick pilot (Cagney) whom she initially hates, but eventually falls in love with.

The press followed the production to the Death Valley location primarily to get a first glimpse of Bette's new husband, and to her delight, Farney handled his initial confrontation with reporters with finesse. He told them that he and Bette tried to divide their time equally between Hollywood and New Hampshire, and that he was newly employed at the Disney Studios, making training films for the Air Force—a job he had secured because of his extensive experience as a flyer.

The Bride Came C.O.D. was greeted warily by the critics; the New York *Times* dismissed it as a "serviceable romp." Davis, lamenting that she and Cagney should have produced something more memorable, called the picture "a truly ridiculous film."

It was around this time that Bette was elected President of the Academy of Motion Pictures Arts and Sciences—the first woman to be so honored. She took her post seriously, but soon learned that she was to serve as a figurehead only. "I was not supposed to preside intelligently. Rather like an heiress at her deceased father's board of director's meeting." Davis resigned the position within a matter of weeks, with her only accomplishment being a suggestion that the annual Oscar awards be held in a theater, with paid admissions, rather than in the nightclubs and banquet rooms where the ceremonies had taken place since 1927.

TOP LEFT: In her first loan-out since *Of Human Bondage*, Davis agreed to star for the Samuel Goldwyn studios in William Wyler's production of *The Little Foxes*, Lillian Hellman's searing drama about a financially—and morally—bankrupt southern family at the turn of the century. Bette would be tackling the role of deadly villainess Regina Giddens, which brought Tallulah Bankhead her greatest triumph during the 1939 Broadway season. Davis had seen and admired the Bankhead performance, but she felt she had something unique to bring to the role, particularly under Wyler's direction and with a screenplay written by Hellman herself.

BOTTOM LEFT: Bette takes a break on the *Little Foxes* set, and her character's imperious attitude is apparent even off-camera. Regina's pinched, suspicious look was achieved by Perc Westmore (who had been imported from Warner Brothers to create Davis' makeup). He narrowed her eyes with false eyelashes, minimized her lip-line for a tight, mean mouth and covered her skin with a chalky white powder. A stickler for detail, Bette loved his efforts. She was not so pleased, however, with the opulent costumes and sets that producer Goldwyn had requested. She felt that the trappings of the Giddens family should be on the seedy side, reflecting their faded glory and precarious financial situation. Goldwyn insisted on Hollywood glamour in the hopes that it would soften the cynical story values and appeal to a wider audience than just the "intellectuals" who were aware of the Hellman play.

Davis' concern over the sets and costumes was nothing as compared to the disagreements she and Wyler had over her interpretation of Regina. He accused Bette of playing the part on one level, strictly as a calculating bitch. He felt that there was a vulnerable side to Regina that she was on constant guard to conceal. Davis saw her only as a monster who intentionally let her husband die in front of her for the sake of his money.

Soon, Wyler and Davis were engaged in shouting matches that were exacerbated by an L.A. heat wave that kept the soundstages sweltering in 100-degree-plus temperatures. In the middle of production, Bette not only walked off the set, but out of the film as well. She rented a house in the resort town of Laguna Beach, while Hollywood gossips reported that Katharine Hepburn would be assuming the Regina role.

In time Davis returned to complete *The Little Foxes*, but her differ-ences with Wyler were only glossed over. She told Whitney Stine, "To be happy to have a film with Wyler as the director finished was indeed a heartbreak for me." The film, despite all of the troubles during its production, was a substantial success, winning great reviews and an Oscar nomination as the year's Best Picture. Bette, too, was nominated for her performance, although she claimed later that her fondest memory connected with *The Little Foxes* came one day on the set. She reminded Samuel Goldwyn—who had just paid a hefty fee for her services—of his reaction ("Who did this to me?") to her 1929 screen test for him. For once, the producer—who was famous for his candid, off-center remarks—was left speechless.

TOP LEFT: Bette followed the turmoil of *The Little Foxes* with *The Man Who Came To Dinner*, the hit Broadway comedy by Kaufman and Hart. She had urged the studio to option the property as a vehicle for herself and John Barrymore, whom she felt would be ideal as the play's title character: pompous and overbearing Sheridan Whiteside. Barrymore was tested for the role, but his failing health made it impossible for him to take on such an assignment. Consequently, the studio imported Monty Wooley from the New York production to recreate his Whiteside performance. On the set, Davis—in character for her role of Whiteside's secretary Maggie—enjoys a laugh with director William Keighley, left, and Wooley.

BOTTOM LEFT: Without a chance to work opposite Barrymore (who died just months after his Whiteside test), Bette's enthusiasm for *The Man Who Came To Dinner* waned, although she still delivered a delightful performance as the put-upon, officious secretary. It was essentially a supporting role, and the critics commended her for making the most of it. The New York *Times* said, "One palm should be handed Bette Davis for accepting the secondary role of the secretary...another palm should be handed her for playing it so moderately and well."

OPPOSITE: Davis poses at Los Angeles' Union Station just prior to embarking on a whistle-stop tour across the country to promote the sale of war bonds. Bette was one of the first Hollywood stars to volunteer her services to the State Department in order to contribute to the war effort.

BELOW: A portrait from Bette's first 1942 film, *In This Our Life*, an improbable melodrama that gave her the most exaggerated bad-girl role yet. As Stanley (!) Timberlake, she leaves her fiance Craig (George Brent) just hours before their wedding in order to run off with the husband (Dennis Morgan) of her mild-mannered sister, Roy (!), played by

BELOW: De Havilland and Davis are captured in a vivid moment from *In This Our Life*. As might be expected, the film's story line, although from a Pulitzer Prize-winning novel, came in for sharp criticism from reviewers —and so did Bette's performance. For the first time, many critics accused her of walking through the role by relying on her familiar mannerisms. Davis herself has called *In This Our Life* "a phony film," although she did enjoy working with her good friend de Havilland and her favorite leading man George Brent. After eleven films, this was the last time Davis and Brent would be co-starred.

OPPOSITE: The splashy ad campaign for *In This Our Life* blatantly appealed to homefront women, millions of whom had made the "woman's picture" more popular in the 1940s than ever.

Olivia de Havilland. Morgan's character is eventually consumed with guilt, and he commits suicide.

Unbelievably, Stanley is forgiven by all concerned until she tries to seduce Craig away from Roy, whom he has fallen in love with. In a rage when Craig turns her down, Stanley accidentally runs down a mother and child. The child is killed, and Stanley tries to pin the rap on the son of her cook (Hattie McDaniel). In a quandary, Stanley then appeals to her uncle (Charles Coburn) until she realizes he has incestuous designs on her. She again takes to the wheel, but while speeding she misses a sharp turn and is killed. The cook's son is exonerated of all suspicion when Craig comes forth and reveals that Stanley was the hit-and-run murderer.

TOP OPPOSITE: Bette signs an autograph at the Hollywood Canteen, the restaurant/nightclub she founded with John Garfield to entertain servicemen who were stationed in, or passing through, Los Angeles. Financed through private and corporate contributions, the Canteen was staffed by volunteers—many with high-glamour profiles. A lucky G.I. might find Hedy Lamarr as his waitress or enjoy a jitterbug with Marlene Dietrich. As president of the enterprise, Davis put in long hours overseeing supply purchasing and organization of the staff. She also frequently performed in skits with other stars, and was occasionally coaxed into song. "The whole idea of the Canteen," she told an interviewer, "was to give the men fun, relaxation and the chance to meet personally and be served by the stars of Hollywood, and not be charged one cent."

BOTTOM OPPOSITE: The Farnsworths enjoy an evening at the Mocambo, Hollywood's favorite nightclub in the Forties. After almost two years, this marriage was still going smoothly, thanks in great part to Farney's refusal to be intimidated by Bette's lofty position as a star. He even shrugged off the occasional moments when he was referred to as "Mr. Davis."

Around this time, Davis had a brief, poignant reunion with Ham Nelson. He was enlisting in the service, and wanted to say goodbye before being shipped overseas. Bette recalled the effect his visit had on her emotions: "Completely irrationally, I was still fond of him. Life does such terrible things to people."

RIGHT: Bette takes time out from her film work and Hollywood Canteen responsibilities to perform in a radio drama. During this busy time, she also wrote an advice column, "What Should I Do?" for *Photoplay* magazine, in which she offered solutions to readers' write-in problems.

TOP RIGHT: An early scene from *Now, Voyager*, in which Bette plays dowdy, repressed Charlotte Vale, a Boston spinster who is helped by a psychiatrist (Claude Rains, pictured) to come out from under the dominance of her unloving mother. After extensive therapy and drastic cosmetic alterations, Charlotte emerges *(bottom)* as a chic, self-possessed woman who unveils her new persona on a luxury cruise. She meets and falls in love with handsome, sensitive Jerry Durrence (Paul Henreid), who is stuck in a miserable marriage with a woman who uses illness to prevent him from leaving her. Realizing Jerry can never be hers, Charlotte returns to Boston, where a sharp confrontation with her mother results in the old woman's death from heart failure. Devastated and guilt-ridden, Charlotte returns to her psychiatrist's retreat and meets a sad, confused little girl who turns out to be Jerry's daughter.

Charlotte and the child form a warm attachment that soon leads to Jerry and Charlotte being reunited — although not in the romantic relationship they both want. Satisfied that, because of his daughter, Jerry will remain an important part of Charlotte's life, she tells him (in one of the most famous closing lines in screen history), "Oh, Jerry, don't let's ask for the moon, we have the stars." *Now, Voyager* was a tremendous success for Bette, winning her another Oscar nomination. She hadn't played a character since Judith in *Dark Victory* that had inspired so much audience sympathy. Surprisingly, she wasn't Jack Warner's first choice for the role of Charlotte Vale; he had his heart set on Irene Dunne for the picture. Davis practically had to beg for the part that she made so unforgettable.

Paul Henreid's Hollywood career was launched brilliantly by his work in *Now, Voyager*. The Austrian actor was imported for the film by producer Hal Wallis, who immediately set about trying to turn him into a slick copy of Charles Boyer. Davis was appalled by Henreid's screen test: "His hair was like patent leather; he also wore a satin smoking jacket. It was obvious he would ruin the picture if allowed to play the part." However, when Bette met him at the studio she realized that, in his natural state, he was ideal casting for Jerry. She intervened on his behalf and insisted that his makeup and costuming be toned down. To this day, Henreid credits Bette with assuring his success in American films.

Henreid's image as a suave lover was established by a small bit of business in the final scene of *Now, Voyager*. Charlotte and Jerry decide to toast their bittersweet reunion with a cigarette. As directed by Irving Rapper, the moment lost its romance through the awkward passing of cigarettes back and forth between the two characters. Henreid came up with the idea of lighting two cigarettes and passing one to Bette —a habit he often shared with his wife. The gesture went into the scene, and when *Now, Voyager* was released in 1942, filmgoers agreed that Paul Henreid lighting two cigarettes was the epitome of Continental sex appeal.

1942
PICTURE "Watch On The Rhine"
NAME BETTE DAVIS
CHARACTER SARA
WARDROBE CHANGE #1
SET WORN IN DAY-COACH IMMIGRATION-STATION
SCENES 1-128 + 50 To 77
DATE TESTED 6-26-42
REMARKS and S.E.
SHUMLIN-GERSTAD-FREDRICKS
SCENE-1E- TAKE 1

OPPOSITE: The wardrobe for *Watch On The Rhine* allowed for little glamour, but Bette was nonetheless happy to be cast as the staunch wife of an anti-Nazi activist in this drama based on Lillian Hellman's play. Davis supplied important support to Paul Lukas as her husband while he risked his life to sabotage Hitler's war machine. *Watch On The Rhine* was nominated for an Academy Award as the Best Picture of 1943, and Lukas was given an Oscar for his performance. The *National Board of Review* magazine saluted Bette for once again taking a supporting role in an important picture: "Bette Davis subdues herself to a secondary role almost with an air of gratitude for being able at last to be uncomplicatedly decent and admirable."

In a nightclub setting, Davis sings "They're Either Too Young or Too Old" to lament the shortage of available men during wartime in *Thank Your Lucky Stars*. The musical was conceived as a showcase for Warner contract players, and it featured such stars as Dinah Shore, John Garfield, Alexis Smith and Hattie McDaniel performing songs—regardless of their individual musical talents. "They're Either Too Young or Too Old" became a surprise novelty hit.

OPPOSITE: Bette's final 1943 release, *Old Acquaintance*, provided her with a character—Kit Marlowe—that she has always claimed was the most like her own personality of any role she has played. *Old Acquaintance* traces the complex relationship between two friends over a twenty-year period. Kit is a down-to-earth writer of "serious books" while Mille (Miriam Hopkins) is a frivolous, selfish woman who takes up writing romantic fiction only because she is envious of Kit's success. Their friendship is complicated by the fact that Mille's long-suffering husband is secretly in love with Kit. This story succeeded primarily because of the casting; *both* stars, it turned out, were playing women they could identify with.

BELOW LEFT: The major confrontation in *Old Acquaintance* comes when Mille rages against Kit, accusing her of trying to steal her husband. Rehearsals for the scene had gone badly, with Hopkins trying her best to

distract and upstage Davis, who refused to get flustered. "I never lost my temper with Miriam on the set," Bette remembers. "I kept it all in until I got home at night. Then I screamed for an hour at least!" Eventually, filming of the scene went smoothly, but Davis realized that she could never work with Hopkins again: "I truly felt sorry for Miriam. She was too good an actress to indulge herself in jealousy of another performer. She finally ruined her career because of this. No one would work with her."

BELOW RIGHT: Davis is the essence of Hollywood's idea of Forties elegance in the final scenes of *Old Acquaintance*. The film had strong appeal for her largely-female following, and was a financial winner. The popularity of her latest picture was, however, little solace for Bette as she faced personal tragedy.

On August 23, 1943, Arthur Farnsworth was headed for a routine business meeting when he suddenly collapsed on Hollywood Boulevard. He was rushed to a nearby hospital with a severe skull fracture. After lingering for a few days in and out of a coma, he died of a cerebral hemorrhage. In her autobiography, Bette said, "It was unbelievable that he was gone—just like that. And so young. It was my first actual experience with death. I was in a state of real shock."

BELOW: Because of speculation that Farnsworth might have been the victim of foul play (he had been involved with secret war work), an inquest was held. Bette testified that approximately four months earlier, Farney had slipped and fallen down a staircase at their Sugar Hill home, but that he had only complained of back pains at the time. The coroner finally decided that he had probably sustained a head injury as well that eventually lead to his death.

OPPOSITE: Although Davis was once again faced with acting a character through several decades, her primary concern about *Mr. Skeffington* was looking the part of the young, vibrantly beautiful Fanny. She told Whitney Stine, "I was far from being beautiful. My genius hairdresser... designed the stunning hairdo I wore as Fanny. It took an hour each morning but was worth it. It gave me the illusion of beauty. Ernest Haller was again my cameraman. He was also responsible for making me beautiful in this film." Even after a decade of stardom, Davis was still insecure about her looks, crediting everyone but herself for her glamorous appearance in *Mr. Skeffington*.

RIGHT: Just a little more than a month following her husband's death, Bette reported to the studio for one of her showiest vehicles, *Mr. Skeffington*, with Claude Rains. She played Fanny Trellis, an enchanting but vain beauty in turn-of-the-century New York who marries Job Skeffington (Rains) for financial security. Marriage, however, does little to curb Fanny's socializing and flirtatious personality. In time, she divorces Skeffington, and even shuns their daughter, whose maturation reminds Fanny of her own advancing age. By the start of World War II, and after several love affairs, she finds herself alone and her beauty ravaged by age and illness. A now-blind Skeffington returns unexpectedly, and because of his condition, Fanny remains forever lovely to him.

RIGHT: This portrait was used to promote *Mr. Skeffington* although it bore little resemblance to Bette's appearance in the period drama. The film received mixed reviews, with many critics praising Davis (". . . as definite a characterization as she has ever profferred") but denouncing the script for its soap-opera slant. Once again Bette was an Oscar nominee for Best Actress.

BELOW: The March 6, 1944 Lux Radio Theatre broadcast reunited Bette with Herbert Marshall to recreate their memorable roles in *The Letter*. Davis was keeping as busy as possible to help overcome the depression she was still feeling over her husband's sudden death.

The success of *Thank Your Lucky Stars* led Warner Brothers to produce another patriotic all-star revue, *Hollywood Canteen*. The thin plot concerned two soldiers who are given royal treatment at the Canteen, and a glimpse of the backstage workings of the club. Several stars, including Bette, played themselves in the picture, but most of the screen time was devoted to songs and dances from Warner regulars. Pictured here are Jack Carson, Jane Wyman, John Garfield and Davis. Joan Crawford, newly-signed to the studio, played a cameo role in the film, but she had no scenes with Bette. Following completion of *Hollywood Canteen*, Davis enjoyed a lengthy vacation during which she visited Washington, D.C. – where she met her idol, President Franklin Roosevelt.

OPPOSITE: As crusading school teacher Miss Lilly Moffat in *The Corn Is Green*, Davis (seen here with Mildred Dunnock) had her first all-out character role since portraying Queen Elizabeth I. Moffat is a plump, middle-aged spinster who moves into a Welsh mining town and sets up a school in her home against great opposition from the suspicious villagers. She sets about educating the young mineworkers, and one in particular (John Dall) shows great natural intelligence. Through Moffat's resolute tutoring, he receives a scholarship from Oxford, but in order to attend the university, he must give up his illegitimate son. Moffat agrees to raise the child, because she feels that nothing should stand in the way of her prize student's higher education.

Critics were impressed with this film version of Emlyn Williams' autobiographical play, and Bette was highly praised for her "subtle, dignified performance." Reviewer E. Arnot Robinson was particularly pleased: "...only Bette Davis, I think, could have combatted so successfully the obvious intention of the adaptors of the play to make frustrated sex the mainspring of (Moffat's) interest in the young miner." A minority of critics compared Davis' work unfavorably to Ethel Barrymore's performance in the Broadway play.

RIGHT: Another radio show brings together this legendary foursome: Bob Hope, Frank Sinatra, Bette and a smitten Jimmy Durante. Davis may have flirted kiddingly with "The Schnozz," but in reality she had just fallen in love with William Grant Sherry, a dashing artist seven years her junior. They had met at a party in Laguna Beach, where Bette was now living year-round.

OPPOSITE: In "Groucho" makeup, Bette signs one of her last autographs at the Hollywood Canteen. With the imminent end of the war, the Canteen—which had brought a glamorous respite to thousands of fighting men—had outlived its usefulness. Today, the site of the Canteen, on Cahuenga Boulevard in Hollywood, is occupied by a multilevel parking structure.

LEFT: A month after they met, Davis and Sherry were married in Riverside, California, on November 29, 1945. The wedding took place in spite of the protestations of Bette's still-influential mother. "Ruthie mistrusted him, as did Bobby," Bette has written. "She so continually criticized him...that she drove me right into his arms. The more Ruthie went on, the more I saw of him."

Bette's relations with her mother and sister had changed since Davis' rise to superstardom. Bobby had suffered through several difficult relationships, and living in the shadow of her sister's accomplishments had taken its toll. At the time of Bette's marriage to Sherry, Bobby was recovering from a severe nervous breakdown. And while there could be no question about Ruthie's devotion to her daughter, she had become a financial drain on Davis even though she, too, had recently remarried. She was the mother of Hollywood's most acclaimed star, and she expected a lifestyle in keeping with her position. Interestingly, Ruthie turned out to be right about William Grant Sherry. He reportedly began abusing Bette—mentally and physically—during the earliest days of their marriage, as they honeymooned in Mexico.

In 1946, Bette founded her own production company, and in partnership with director Curtis Bernhardt, chose to produce *A Stolen Life* as her first project. A remake of a 1939 British film that had starred Elisabeth Bergner, *A Stolen Life* gave Davis the chance to play twins for the first time; she was Kate, the sensitive introverted artist, and Pat, the lively glamour girl.

Kate falls in love with handsome Bill Emerson (Glenn Ford, pictured) but he is dazzled by Pat, and marries her. Several months later, Pat is drowned in a boating accident, and Kate assumes her identity. After a series of predictable complications, Bill forgives Kate's masquerade and realizes he has ended up with the sister who was right for him all along.

OPPOSITE: Davis is thoughtful on the set of *A Stolen Life*. Production on this picture did not run smoothly. Bette and co-producer/director Bernhardt had several heated arguments over Davis' wardrobe, Glenn Ford's haircut and various other major and minor aspects of filming. Bette's first producing venture turned out to be her last. "... I was no more allowed to be a real producer than the man in the moon," she said. "As star in a dual role, I simply meddled as usual. If that was producing, I had been a mogul for years."

A Stolen Life proved to be a popular moneymaker, but most critics greeted it with scorn. The New York *Times* said, "It is a distressingly empty piece of show-off for the multi-Oscar winner to perform and, at that, a quite painful presentation of the talented actress' gaits." There were words of praise, however, for the process shots in the film that allowed Bette to appear as both twins on screen at the same time.

TOP LEFT: Bette was once again in Paul Henreid's arms in *Deception*, a romantic triangle set against the world of classical music. Out of love for her husband (Henreid), Bette murders her ex-lover (Claude Rains), a great composer/conductor, to prevent him from ruining the comeback concert of Henreid, who is newly-returned from a concentration camp. The film was a success with both the critics and the public.

During production of this picture, Davis discovered she was pregnant, prompting studio wits to refer to the film as *Conception*. On May 1, 1947, Bette gave birth to a daughter, whom she named Barbara Davis Sherry. The new mother, who was thirty-nine, was informed by her doctors that she would not be able to have any more children.

BOTTOM LEFT: Four months after Barbara's birth, Davis began filming *Winter Meeting*, a two-character study about an emotionally-unfulfilled poetess and her feeble romance with a war hero (Jim Davis, pictured) who is struggling with his desire to become a priest. Taken from the highly-regarded book by Ethel Vance, *Winter Meeting* emerged on the screen as a talky, unfocussed bore. Bette refers to it as "a dreary film," and it was a financial flop. Thirty years later, Jim Davis finally achieved stardom as Jock Ewing on TV's *Dallas*.

OPPOSITE: April 1948, Barbara Davis Sherry (or B.D. as she was nicknamed) is presented to press photographers by her parents following her christening in San Clemente, California. Davis rejoiced in being with her daughter during this time, but she was on constant guard with Sherry because of his violent tendencies. Bette was extremely careful about keeping B.D. out of her father's way when his mood turned surly, and although she was grateful that the union had produced her daughter, she knew that the marriage would not survive for long. In 1962 Davis wrote, "I'm afraid in Sherry's case he had decided he was the King. He crowned himself. I wanted to do the same thing many times—crown him."

BELOW: For her first comedy in seven years, Bette joined Robert Montgomery in *June Bride*, a clever battle-of-the-sexes story that also served as a witty send-up of "women's magazines." In the story, Davis is a high-powered editor who turns a "typical American family" upside down when she stages a June wedding (in the dead of winter) for

BELOW: Wearing a "black fright wig" and an Edith Head-designed peasant blouse, Bette takes a cigarette break on the set of *Beyond The Forest*, her final release of the decade and the last film she made under her Warner Brothers contract. In a role she was ten years too old for, Davis played Rosa Moline, "a twelve-o'clock girl in a nine-o'clock town," who is discontent with her marriage to Joseph Cotten and their routine lives in a colorless Wisconsin industrial hamlet. She dreams of running off to Chicago to become the wife of wealthy industrialist David Brian. During the course of the melodramatic story, Rosa seduces Brian (who promptly rejects her), becomes pregnant, murders a man who threatens to tell Brian of her condition, induces a miscarriage and finally dies as she is crawling toward the railroad tracks in the fever-induced delusion that she can make it to Chicago.

the benefit of a magazine feature. Montgomery is her chauvinistic ex-lover and reluctant assistant.

In the tradition of almost all 1940s films about ambitious businesswomen, Bette realizes the folly of her ways by the end of the picture and decides to abandon her hard-earned career in favor of becoming Montgomery's doting wife. *June Bride* was hailed as a welcome change of pace from Davis by most critics, and it was a moderate box-office success.

OPPOSITE: During a break in *June Bride* filming, Bette joins Gary Cooper in accepting awards representing the two stars' popularity in France. The *La Belle France* statuettes were awarded to Davis and Cooper after they had won a poll taken by a number of French newspapers.

RIGHT: A ridiculous publicity still from a ridiculous movie. *Beyond The Forest* was unquestionably the most inferior picture Davis had made since becoming a star, and it brought her glory days at Warner Brothers to an ignominious end. For almost five years, Bette's vehicles at the studio had been deteriorating in quality, and although she had survived several (sometimes indifferent) production regimes, it was now clear that even Jack Warner was no longer supportive of her projects.

The financial panic that swept the film industry in the late Forties resulted in the studios dropping several major stars whose films were not as profitable as they had been a decade earlier. Warner was no exception. The executives now considered Bette something of a dinosaur, regardless of the prestige she had brought the studio during her reign as queen of the lot.

OPPOSITE: There was also the sticky problem of her age. Davis was now forty, and it became increasingly difficult to find suitable scripts for her. *Beyond The Forest* proved embarrassingly that playing younger than her age was a disservice to Bette and her audiences—and she hated doing it. "People get the idea that actresses my age are dying to play younger women," she told Hedda Hopper. "The fact is we die every time we play them."

After several weeks of bitter haggling with the front office, Bette (in the midst of filming *Beyond The Forest*) flatly told Jack Warner that she would walk off the picture if she wasn't released from her contract. He acquiesced, and after almost eighteen years, Davis and the studio agreed to a "professional divorce."

Fortunately, Bette's services were sought after elsewhere, and her first assignment as a free-lance actress was at RKO, where she filmed *The Story of a Divorce* under the direction of Curtis Bernhardt. The picture was made in the fall of 1949, but the studio was unsure about its quality, so it sat on the shelf for almost two years. More bad news came with the reviews of *Beyond The Forest*—both the film and Davis' performance received scathing notices. Some critics went so far as to suggest that her career in films might be over. What was *definitely* over was Bette's marriage to William Grant Sherry—she had filed for divorce in July. This unpleasant time might have served

as a portent for Davis: with one striking exception (just months away), the 1950s would prove to be the most painful period in her life, both personally and professionally. She would later refer to the upcoming decade as "ten black years."

THE
FIFTIES
AND
SIXTIES

Hugh Marlowe, Gary Merrill and Bette prepare for a difficult scene on the set of *All About Eve*, the classic comedy-drama about the dark side of the New York theater. The film supplied Davis with, arguably, her most memorable role as Margo Channing, a temperamental, glamorous, sometimes neurotic Broadway star facing middle age and aggressive competition from Eve Harrington (Anne Baxter), a ruthless young actress who insinuates herself into Margo's life.

OPPOSITE: In retrospect it is almost impossible to imagine any other actress on earth playing Margo. But Davis was not the first choice of producer Darryl Zanuck for the coveted part. He had signed Claudette Colbert, but just days before production was scheduled to commence, she suffered a serious back injury and had to withdraw from the project. In a panic, Zanuck sent the script to Bette, who was finishing up filming on *The Story of a Divorce*.

Even a cursory perusal of Joseph Mankiewicz's screenplay convinced Davis that this was the role, and the film, she had been longing for. She said later, "When I finished reading *All About Eve* I was on cloud nine. That night I met Mankiewicz (who would also be directing the film) for dinner to discuss wardrobe. He told me that Margo Channing was the kind of dame who would treat her mink coat like a poncho!" This seemingly minor insight gave Bette the "handle" she needed to bring Margo unforgettably to life. Once filming began, Mankiewicz had nothing but praise for Davis: "...Bette was letter perfect. She was *syllable* perfect. There was no fumbling for words; they'd become hers—as Margo Channing."

TOP LEFT: Gary Merrill, Gregory Ratoff and Davis in the wonderful cocktail party sequence in *All About Eve*, which contains some of Mankiewicz's most biting dialogue. At the beginning of this scene, Margo delivers one of the most famous lines in film history as she warns her guests, "Fasten your seat belts. It's going to be a bumpy night." Later, after she has consumed more than a few martinis, a morose Margo brings the party to a standstill by insisting that the somber *Lieberstraum* be played repeatedly on the piano. Bill Sampson (Merrill) tells her, "Many of your guests have been wondering when they may be permitted to view the body. Where has it been laid out?" Looking drunkenly up from her cocktail, Margo answers "It hasn't been laid out. We haven't finished with the embalming. As a matter of fact, you're looking at it. The remains of Margo Channing—sitting up." In another scene, she is in the midst of a heated argument with playwright Lloyd Richards (Marlowe) when he tells her that she should act only in plays written by authors who have been dead for three hundred years. Margo shouts at him, "*All* playwrights should be dead for three hundred years!"

As refreshing and sophisticated as the dialogue in *All About Eve* was, it was only one of several elements that made the film a charmed experience for everyone involved in its production. The casting (even down to Marilyn Monroe's delightful small part as a graduate of the "Copacabana School of Dramatic Arts") was flawless, and Mankiewicz's insightful direction elicited splendid performances from all of the acting talent (with the possible exception of Gary Merrill, who tended toward hamminess in several key scenes). Merrill's romantic chemistry with Bette was potent, however, and after just a few days of filming it became obvious to everyone that this chemistry was proving to be just as potent *off* screen.

BOTTOM LEFT: Davis and Merrill were extremely attracted to each other practically from the moment they met during pre-production. Davis biographer Charles Higham characterized this attraction from Bette's point of view: "Drawn always to physical men who were unpretty and rugged, Bette was captivated by Merrill...he was her match in temperament if not in talent; her match

in his drive and fierce commitment to his profession, his intelligence and understanding." Just months after their first meeting, Davis and Merrill were married in Juarez, Mexico on July 28, 1950–three weeks after Bette's divorce from Sherry had become final.

ABOVE: Ruthie accompanies her daughter to the world premiere of *All About Eve* at Grauman's Chinese Theater in Hollywood on November 9, 1950. Critical reaction to the film was nothing short of ecstatic. The New York *Morning Telegraph* raved, "*All About Eve*... is probably the wittiest, the most devastating, the most adult and literate motion picture ever made that had anything to do with the New York stage." The paper went on to call Bette's work "...the finest,

most compelling, and the most perceptive performance she has ever played out on the screen."

Critics who had just months earlier lambasted Davis in *Beyond The Forest* (and despaired about her future in movies), now called her creation of the petulant, gifted, exasperating Margo Channing one of the most indelible characterizations ever put on film. There seemed no doubt that Bette would be an Oscar recipient for her celebrated performance in *All About Eve*, which was proving to be a box-office sensation.

117

As part of her national radio show, flamboyant columnist Hedda Hopper interviewed Bette on the heels of her triumph in *Eve*. Hopper told her audience, "Hollywood's most thrilling comeback in 1950 was made by its finest actress, Bette Davis. For my money, her performance in *All About Eve* topped anything she ever did."

There was much conjecture about who had served as inspiration for Bette's interpretation of Margo Channing. The name most often mentioned was Tallulah Bankhead. For years it was reported that Bankhead held a grudge against Davis for starring in the film versions of some of Tallulah's greatest stage successes. Now, gossips insisted, Bette was gleefully parodying Bankhead in her playing of Margo. Davis has always denied this, claiming that her main source of inspiration for the role was Elisabeth Bergner. "Tallulah herself," Bette has said, "more than anyone else, accused me of imitating her as Margo Channing." Bankhead was never convinced that Bette-as-Margo was not a wicked send-up of *her*; among friends she always referred to the movie as *All About Me*.

OPPOSITE: Several days after the opening of *All About Eve*, Davis takes part in a hallowed Hollywood tradition by placing her signature (and hand and foot prints) in cement for posterity in the forecourt of the Chinese Theater.

OPPOSITE: Bette and Gary Merrill make one of their first Hollywood appearances as a married couple. Davis spoke of her fourth husband in reflective terms: "I sensed in Gary my last chance at love and marriage. I wanted these as desperately as ever. I had been an actress first and a woman second." Curiously, Margo Channing expresses similar sentiments about Bill Sampson, Merrill's character in *All About Eve*.

Shortly after his marriage to Bette, Merrill had to spend several weeks in the Virgin Islands working on a film. During his absence, Davis rented a home in Connecticut large enough to accommodate the growing Merrill family. Prior to their wedding, Bette and Gary had decided to adopt a child, and while Merrill was out of the country, Davis welcomed an infant daughter. She was named Margot in honor of the character that had brought her new parents together. Bette was delighted to present her baby to B.D. "When I walked in the house," she has said, "I told her to close her eyes, I had a present for her. I put a real live doll in her little arms. Her eyes, when she opened them, had all the wonders of the universe. She had a sister." Sadly, the euphoria surrounding Margot's adoption would be short-lived.

RIGHT: As Joseph Mankiewicz looks on, Bette displays the scroll she has just been presented by the New York Film Critics for her performance in *All About Eve*. "Finally I had been given an award by the New York Film Critics," Davis said. "To all of us in Hollywood this award seemed to be a special compliment." Shortly after this ceremony, the Academy Award nominations were announced, and *All About Eve* received a record fourteen nominations, including a nod for Bette as the year's Best Actress.

Unexpectedly, 1950 turned out to be a highly competitive year for movie actresses. Bette's brilliant work was matched by Gloria Swanson's hypnotic performance in *Sunset Boulevard*—the *real* comeback story

of the year. Davis also found herself up against her talented *Eve* costar, Anne Baxter. The surprise winner of the Oscar, however, turned out to be Judy Holliday for her unique comic performance in *Born Yesterday*. Bette was, of course, disappointed—but she took solace in *Eve*'s victory as Best Picture, her new marriage, and the renewed impetus of her career.

OPPOSITE: Capitalizing on the success of *All About Eve*, RKO president Howard Hughes finally released *The Story of a Divorce* under a new title, *Payment On Demand*. Essentially a character study of a middle-aged woman facing the break-up of her twenty-year marriage, the script offered Davis another opportunity to play several different periods in her character's life. Through flashbacks, she is the young, supportive bride of Barry Sullivan, and later *(above)* the elegant matron to whom social climbing is an all-consuming passion.

Bette was unhappy with the film's title change; she felt that *Payment On Demand* indicated a story about kidnapping or blackmail. She was also not pleased with the new ending that Hughes had insisted be filmed before he would release the picture. In the original closing scenes, Bette's character is unwilling to alter her

ambitious personality to perhaps save her marriage. The ending of the film as released is softer-edged, leaving the viewer with the impression that the estranged couple will get back together. *Payment on Demand* fared well at the box office, and Davis was praised for the subtlety of her work. The Los Angeles *Times* said, "This is no such flashy performance as she gave in *All About Eve*. It is much finer-grained."

BELOW: The positive afterglow of Bette's triumph in *All About Eve* began dimming seriously with her first 1952 release, *Another Man's Poison*. The screenplay reunited Davis (seen here with Anthony Steele) and Gary Merrill, but it was a melodramatic hodge-podge about a mystery writer who murders her escaped-convict husband, attempts to murder his fellow escapee, and

finally dies from taking poison she is given accidentally.

Filming in England (under the direction of *Dark Victory's* Irving Rapper) was not a pleasant experience for Bette. The British press was unkind about her "matronly" appearance, and there was more than one reference to Merrill as "Mr. Davis." "We had nothing but...trouble," she said. "Gary and I often wondered why we agreed to make this film after we got started working on it." Reviews of *Another Man's Poison* were decidedly mixed, with many critics accusing Bette of scenery-chewing and once again relying on her patented theatrics. The film was not a financial success.

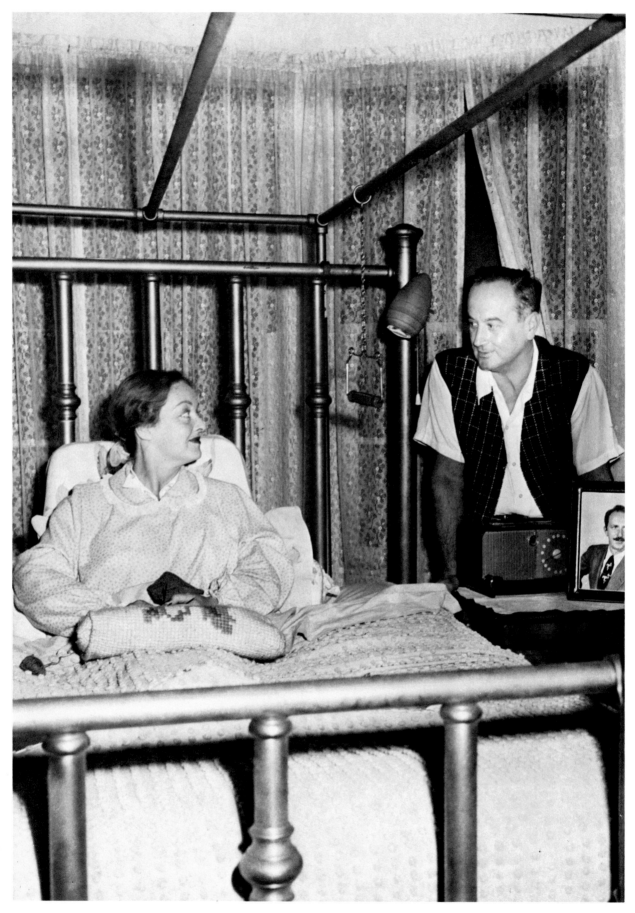

OPPOSITE: Soon after Bette's return to Hollywood, she decided, surprisingly, to play a small-but-interesting part in Gary Merrill's new film for Twentieth Century-Fox, *Phone Call From A Stranger*. Cast as a bedridden invalid, Davis confers here with director Jean Negulesco about an upcoming scene. The framed photo on Bette's nightstand is of Keenan Wynn, who, along with Merrill, Shelley Winters and Michael Rennie, rounded out the picture's cast. *Phone Call From A Stranger* was a moderate success, and several critics saluted Davis for her willingness to accept a role based on quality rather than size.

RIGHT: In a carefully-posed publicity photo, Bette (as washed-up movie star Margaret Elliot) is comforted by rugged Sterling Hayden in *The Star*, an exploitative film about the depressing decline of an Oscar-winning actress. Filmed in less than a month, *The Star* is little more than a Hollywood cliché, but it did offer Davis a strong role, for which she won another Academy Award nomination. During the brief production, Bette established a warm friendship with fourteen-year-old Natalie Wood, who played her daughter.

The Star was not a moneymaker, despite decent reviews. One moment from the film, however, has become classic and is usually shown during TV tributes to Davis: a despairing Margaret grabs her Academy Award and shouts, "Come on Oscar, let's you and me get drunk!" Following *The Star*, Bette made an unwise decision: she refused the lead in the movie version of the Broadway play, *Come Back, Little Sheba*. Shirley Booth got the role and won an Oscar for her touching performance. Davis later called her turn-down of this part, "one of the really great mistakes of my career."

BELOW: September 1952. While composer Vernon Duke accompanies her, Bette rehearses one of her songs in the musical revue *Two's Company*, set to open a month later on Broadway. With her movie career at another frustrating low point, Davis agreed to return to the stage in this show, primarily because of its remarkable production team. Duke's music would be complemented with lyrics by Ogden Nash and Sammy Cahn, Jerome Robbins was handling the choreography, the skits were being directed by Jules Dassin, and the entire show was under the supervision of John Murray Anderson—whose acting school Bette had attended so successfully in the late Twenties.

Bette's return to Broadway was originally conceived as a follow-up to Judy Garland's record-breaking comeback engagement at the Palace Theater a year earlier. Unfortunately, like many of Garland's ventures, *Two's Company* was plagued with strife from the first rehearsal. There were the usual shouting matches over "creative differences," but more alarming were the out-of-town tryouts; Davis collapsed from exhaustion several times, once in the middle of a number on stage. Broadway gossip indicated that the show would close shortly after its ballyhooed opening at the Alvin Theater. Bette wrote of the experience, "The (opening night) ovation was, to say the least, heartwarming. The reviews were bloodcurdling. I lived on Dexadrine and shots during the run, always exhausted. The houses were full—that was a comfort . . . I had fun doing the show and most of the audience had fun seeing the tragedienne Bette Davis making fun of herself."

OPPOSITE: Resembling a female impersonator, Davis makes an entrance as Sadie Thompson in the "Roll Along, Sadie" number from *Two's Company*. Thanks to standing-room-only business, Bette continued in the show for several months, until she discovered that her chronic exhaustion was caused by poison in her system from an advanced case of osteomyelitis of the jaw. She underwent complicated surgery, and was forced into a lengthy recuperation period.

This difficult time was made much worse when columnist Walter Winchell reported to his national radio audience that Bette was *really* suffering from cancer of the jaw. Gary Merrill had to threaten legal action to get Winchell to retract his story, and although there was an apology of sorts, the cancer story clung to Davis for several years. More unhappiness suddenly struck the Merrill family when it was learned that Margot was brain-damaged. Bette recalls, "It was a bitter blow and an enormous heartbreak to Gary and me . . . B.D. once said to a friend over the phone, 'My sister has a broken head.'" Margot had to be placed in a special school, and to this day remains institutionalized. This tragic situation was made only slightly more bearable by the presence of the baby boy the Merrills had adopted several months earlier. He was named Michael, and he proved to be a great comfort to Bette during this depressing period.

OPPOSITE: Davis is animated as she prepares to resume her movie career in 1955. She had spent three years away from Hollywood recovering from illness, mothering her young children, encouraging Gary Merrill's busy film and TV career and otherwise enjoying her beloved New England. She was now refreshed and eager to return to work, but found herself filled with self-doubts after signing with Twentieth Century-Fox to once again play Queen Elizabeth I in the studio's big-budgeted, color epic, *Sir Walter Raleigh*.

TOP RIGHT: On the set of *The Virgin Queen* (as *Sir Walter Raleigh* had since been retitled), Bette poses alongside her chair, which has been autographed by well-wishing members of the cast and crew. Davis said, "I was sure of nothing. Least of all myself. The first day was a nightmare for me. (But) after the first take was printed, I relaxed."

BOTTOM RIGHT: Marlon Brando (clutching the Oscar he had just won as Best Actor) seems delighted to pose with Bette, who presented the award to him at the 1955 Academy Award ceremonies. Davis' unusual headpiece caused comment until she revealed that she was in the midst of *Virgin Queen* filming and had once again shaved off her eyebrows and hairline to portray Elizabeth I. Bette's appearance on this Oscar program brought her great joy when her entrance was greeted with a wildly enthusiastic ovation. "I was being welcomed by the town where I had spent most of my life," she said. "I couldn't keep the tears from my eyes. The applause went on and on. It was one of the greatest moments of my career."

The Virgin Queen pitted Bette against Joan Collins (as Beth, Elizabeth's lady-in-waiting) in competition for the attentions of Sir Walter Raleigh, played by British actor Richard Todd. During the course of the film, Raleigh decides to marry Beth, but by doing so he incurs the wrath of Queen Elizabeth, who has him executed.

Most critics found *The Virgin Queen* to be excellent historical drama, and they agreed with Bette's assessment of her performance: "I really think this Elizabeth was finer than my first." The Los Angeles *Examiner* proclaimed, "Miss Davis injects life and action into the tale, seeming to inspire everyone and everything around her. What a queen! What an actress!" Davis convinced Fox to stage the picture's premiere in Portland, Maine to benefit the local children's theater. *The Virgin Queen* was not a box-office hit. Bette blames the studio's shoddy advertising campaign, which featured an incongruous illustration of Davis as Margo Channing.

OPPOSITE: After a brief rest in Portland, Bette reported to Columbia studios to play a principled New England librarian in *Storm Center*. Because she refuses to remove a book about communism from her shelves, Alicia Hull (Davis) is fired by a small-minded, paranoid city council. It takes the burning of the library to convince the small town that book banning is undesirable, and Hull is vindicated.

Typical of several mid-Fifties movies rejecting the witch-hunt mentality so prevalent just five years earlier, *Storm Center* fails to make a strong impact because of the implausibility of several story points, and also because Davis—due partly to the script—does not inspire much audience sympathy for her put-upon character. Columbia delayed the release of the picture for several months, by which time Bette had completed and released another film.

The intriguing cast of *The Catered Affair*–Davis, Ernest Borgnine, Debbie Reynolds, and Barry Fitzgerald–get together for a typical MGM group portrait. For her role of Aggie Hurley, the frumpy wife of Bronx-cabbie Borgnine, Bette is wearing an unflattering wig and several pounds of padding–although she was actually a little plump during this period. Based on a TV play by Paddy Chayefsky, *The Catered Affair* was intended as an unofficial follow-up to the previous year's surprise smash, *Marty*, which had won Borgnine a Best Actor Oscar.

The story is an earthy domestic drama about a simple, inarticulate family that faces the dilemma of how to best spend their small savings–on a cab for the hard-working father, or on a traditional wedding for their only daughter. All ends well when the purchase of the cab is made possible because the daughter decides on a simple, inexpensive ceremony.

Although it never attained the popularity of *Marty*, *A Catered Affair* succeeded in touching its audiences primarily because of the committed performances of the actors. Borgnine, playing years older than his actual age, is fine as a man who is frustrated in his efforts to provide a better life for his family. He keeps his emotions to himself (except when drinking), and he goes for years without telling his patient wife that he loves her. Debbie Reynolds as the daughter is impressive in her first dramatic role, and Barry Fitzgerald (in his last performance) is perfect as a pouty Irish uncle.

As for Bette, *The New Yorker* review said, "In the role of the mother, (she) is done up to resemble a fat and slovenly housewife, but even so she conveys the impression that she's really a dowager doing a spot of slumming in the Bronx." Other reviews were more positive, and the performance was particularly well thought of in Britain. Davis considers the role "one of my proudest efforts as an actress." This is probably one of those instances when a veteran actor's familiarity works against the credibility of an unusual performance. Had this been Bette's first screen appearance, it is likely that critics would have found little fault with her work.

OPPOSITE: May 1957, Bette returns to the Warner lot for the first time in years to visit Gary Merrill, who is making a film for the studio. With their mother are B.D. and Michael. Hollywood gossips were now circulating stories about trouble in the Merrill marriage. It was claimed that some of the tension stemmed from the fact that Merrill was now working more consistently than his wife.

Just a month after this photo was taken, Bette faced another, sudden health crisis. She was exploring her new home in the Brentwood section of Los Angeles, when she stepped through a door that she had been told led to a closet. It led instead to a darkened basement. Bette fell twenty feet and landed on concrete flooring. She suffered a broken back and multiple deep bruises. Miraculously, she healed rapidly and was appearing on television just six months after the fall.

TOP RIGHT: Film roles became scarce for Bette following *A Catered Affair*, and for three years she turned to television for work. Here, she appears in a Daphne du Maurier-scripted episode on NBC's mystery anthology, *Suspicion*, aired in April 1958. Davis had appeared semi-regularly on the home screen since 1952. She knew that keeping herself before the public in any medium helped to reinforce her stardom and served to alert film producers that she was not retired. During this period, Bette acted in dozens of TV shows, including an Alfred Hitchcock episode that reunited her with Frank Albertson, who had costarred with her in 1932's *Way Back Home*.

BOTTOM RIGHT: Davis performs a spirited can-can as the title character in "The Elizabeth McQueeny Story," a segment of *Wagon Train*, a popular western TV series. Bette played a salty saloon hostess in this 1959 program that was intended as a pilot, but never was developed into a series. This marked the first time Davis had appeared in a story set in the old west.

OPPOSITE: An unusual portrait of Bette highlights the short hairstyle she wore during the last months of the 1950s. She chose this cut partly because it was comfortable under the sometimes heavy wigs she was required to wear for the character roles that (at this time) were all she was being offered.

Bette returned to films in a cameo role as Russia's Catherine the Great in *John Paul Jones* starring Robert Stack (pictured). The movie was made in Italy, and Davis brought B.D. and Bobby along for an impromptu vacation. This film was only spottily distributed in the United States, with many of Bette's scenes deleted from the final print. "If you sneezed while watching it," Bette remarked, "I had disappeared!"

She did not fare much better with her next project, *The Scapegoat*, in which she was cast as Alec Guinness' cigar-smoking mother. Bette and Guinness are seen here during pre-production on the English location. In spite of a story by Daphne du Maurier and a screenplay prepared by Gore Vidal, *The Scapegoat* emerged as nothing more than a showcase for Guinness in a dual role. The award-winning actor was initially concerned that Bette (who was his contemporary) would not photograph old enough to be believable as his mother. "I assure you, Mr. Guinness," she told him, "that when I am properly made up, I will look old enough. . ."

OPPOSITE: Sure enough, *The Scapegoat* presented filmgoers with a decrepit Bette Davis who appeared at least twenty years older than her actual age. Critics were kind to her when the picture was released in the summer of 1959, but the public perceived *The Scapegoat* as an art film and it did not attract a large audience.

As the Fifties drew to a close, Bette looked forward to her future with trepidation. Personally, she now had to admit that there *were* major problems in her marriage and her (once great) career as an actress seemed mired in supporting roles, mostly on television. At this time, she would not have dared dream that in less than three years she would be back on top as one of Hollywood's most sought-after stars.

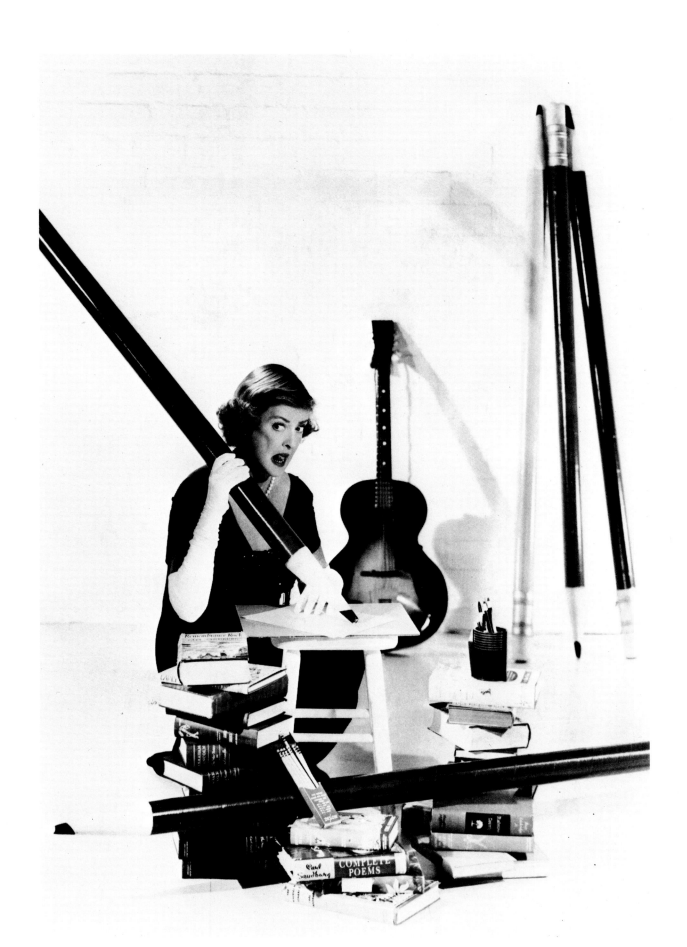

OPPOSITE: For the 1959-60 theatrical season, Bette and Gary Merrill agreed to tour the country in *The World of Carl Sandburg*, an evening of dramatic readings culled from the honored author's works. Davis had not considered returning to the stage since her painful experience in *Two's Company*, but this project appealed to her because she was a devout Sandburg fan, and because she hoped that a joint venture might improve the status of her by now rapidly-failing marriage. To publicize the seventy-city tour, Bette posed for a series of photographs, including this one, that can only be described as camp.

TOP LEFT: During an appearance in New Jersey to promote the tour, Bette is presented with a portrait by Joel Kudler, a devoted young admirer. To her delight, Davis realized that Kudler represented a new generation of fans who were not even born when she was reigning as Hollywood's queen. Thanks to television, millions of young people were becoming as familiar with Bette as their parents had been. Her regular guestings on various series accounted for some of this popularity, but it was primarily the airing of her old films that was garnering new audiences. Unlike the performances of so many of Bette's contemporaries, her best work didn't seem dated. Her insistence on realism, and her willingness to forego glamour for the sake of a character role, kept most of her performances from the Thirties and Forties fresh and appealing decades later.

BOTTOM LEFT: When *The World of Carl Sandburg* reached Los Angeles, it was booked into the newly-named Huntington Hartford theater, a venue that Bette felt particularly comfortable in—she had performed on its stage several times in the 1940s, when it served as the home of the Lux Radio Theatre. The tour was exhilarating for Davis as an actress: "It was like playing the full range of every part I'd ever done, in fragments, during one evening."

The Hollywood opening was a sensation; dozens of celebrities turned out to wish Bette well, and she was given roaring ovations throughout the performance. The Hollywood *Citizen News* noted, "Miss Davis deserved most of this applause, even if this particular audience came primed to pay her homage."

The Merrills were thrilled when Sandburg congratulated them following the L.A. performance. In a curtain speech, he said to Bette, "I would salute you not only for your genius but for endurance." The evening was a triumph for Davis, made richer because Ruthie was in the front row—as she had been for every one of her daughter's stage appearances for over forty years. *The World of Carl Sandburg* moved on to Broadway, but it did not enjoy a long run. Reviews were mixed, and there was criticism about the lack of chemistry between Bette and her new leading man, Leif Erickson.

Gary Merrill had dropped out of the tour in San Francisco in May, immediately following Bette's announcement that she was filing for divorce, citing cruelty. Contrary to Davis' hopes, her marriage had not been helped by the togetherness the tour necessitated. Instead, her differences with Merrill became more aggravated. Insiders claimed that the Merrill union had been spoiled by the clash of two oversized actor's egos and the inherent insecurities and self-involvement. There were also reports that Gary had developed a drinking problem.

Bette was discreet about the reasons for the break-up, although she did write cryptically about it several months after the divorce was granted: "I am sure I have been uncompromising, peppery, intractable, monomaniacal, tactless, volatile and oftimes disagreeable. I stand accused of it all. But at forty I allowed the female to take over. It was too late. I admit Gary broke my heart. He killed the dream forever. The little woman no longer exists."

Bette and John F. Kennedy are photographed at a Democratic fundraiser in October 1960, and it is unclear who is receiving whose autograph. Amusingly, Bette—who was entering her fourth decade of worldwide fame—was required to wear a name tag!

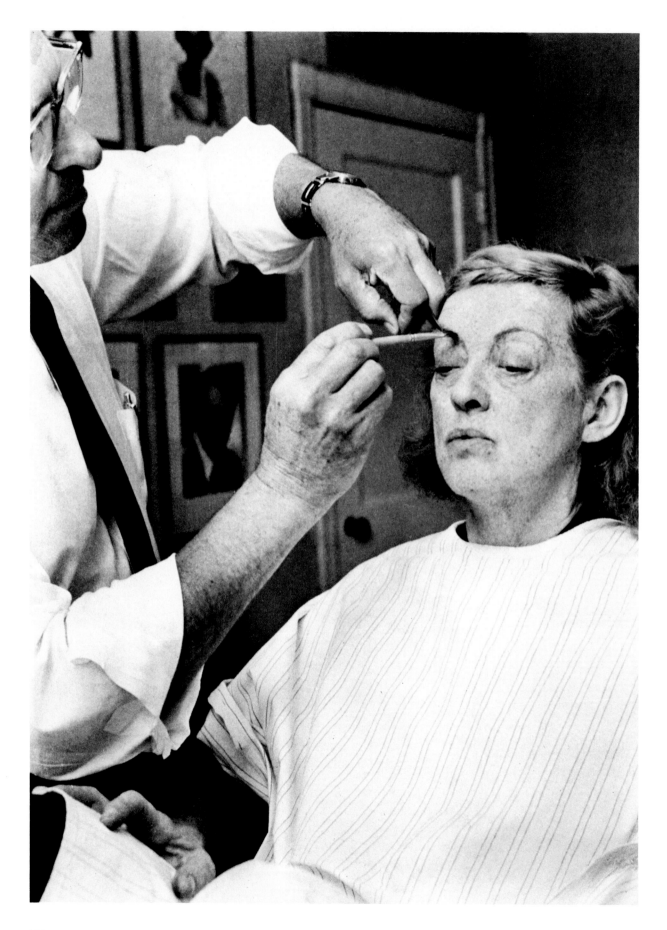

OPPOSITE: In preparation for her first film in two years, Davis submits to unflattering makeup in order to portray Apple Annie, a tattered character who peddles apples on Broadway—when she isn't stinking drunk. The film, *Pocketful of Miracles*, was director Frank Capra's remake of his 1933 comedy-drama *Lady for a Day*, based on characters created by Damon Runyon. Capra originally wanted Helen Hayes to play Annie, but when she became unavailable, he approached Bette—who was not, at first, receptive to the idea. She finally agreed to take the role after B.D. read the script and told her, "Mother, you'd be the best Apple Annie in the world!"

RIGHT: *Pocketful of Miracles* tells the fairy-tale-like story of a group of Twenties hoods and hangers-on who help the grimy-but-lovable Annie masquerade as Mrs. E. Worthington Manville, an elegant Park Avenue dowager, so that she will be acceptable to her long-absent daughter (played by Ann-Margret in her film debut), who is returning to New York as the fianceé of a wealthy European.

Bette as the transformed Apple Annie. The *Pocketful of Miracles* screenplay may have been sweetly sentimental, but the production was, according to Capra, ". . . shaped in the fires of discord and filmed in an atmosphere of pain, strain and loathing." There was a great deal of tension between Davis and the film's lead, Glenn Ford. Shortly after filming began, Ford told a reporter that it was he who had arranged for Bette to work in the film. He boasted about engineering Davis' "comeback" out of gratitude for the career boost he had enjoyed after costarring with her in *A Stolen Life* fifteen years earlier. When Bette heard about the interview, she was livid: "Who is that son of a bitch that he should say he helped me have a *comeback*! That shitheel wouldn't have helped me out of a sewer."

OPPOSITE: *Pocketful of Miracles* was released for the Christmas 1961 season, and it emerged as an entertaining, if old-fashioned, movie. None of the on-set hassles were evident on screen. Critics hailed Bette's exuberant performance as Annie, although some felt that her transition to Mrs. E. Worthington Manville was too easily accomplished. Audiences responded to Davis and the picture with misty eyes, and it was a box-office success.

Bette does not, however, look back fondly at *Pocketful of Miracles*. Not only was the filming an unpleasant professional experience, but she suffered a great personal loss when Ruthie died at seventy-six shortly before production on the film was completed. Bette and Bobby were devastated, and at the time Davis wrote, "It seemed impossible. Her vitality, her joy were gone forever. Her protection and her dependency, her wisdom and her little-girlness and her guts." Davis' relationship with her mother had gone through many phases over the years, but Ruthie's devotion to her daughter's career never wavered. For the tombstone, Bette supplied this inscription: "Ruthie—you will always be in the front row."

Davis was helped through her

grief by having to meet two immediate challenges. She had signed with Putnam to write her autobiography (with only a few months to meet her manuscript deadline), and —surprisingly—she agreed to return to the Broadway stage for the 1961-62 season in Tennessee Williams' new drama, *The Night of the Iguana*.

Bette as Maxine Falk, the free-thinking, pot-smoking landlady of a run-down resort hotel in *The Night of the Iguana*, which went into rehearsal in the fall of 1961. The play had a rough gestation period. Although pleased to be playing a character with a strong sexual aura for the first time in years, Davis was not in a positive frame of mind during the entire *Iguana* project. She was distracted by several thorny problems.

She was embroiled in a bitter fight with Gary Merrill over his visitation rights to their son Michael. Bette wanted all rights revoked because she reportedly felt that Merrill's heavy drinking was a poor influence on the child. She was also constantly bickering with her editor at Putnam over various aspects of her book, and, of course, she was still grieving over the death of her mother.

Additionally, Davis was not getting along well with her costars in the play. She was convinced that Margaret Leighton and Patrick O'Neal considered her an inferior stage actor and resented her larger-than-life stardom. The latter must surely have been true, as Bette's fans disrupted almost every performance from the beginning of tryouts with noisy applause following even her briefest scenes, often sabotaging the concentration of the other performers on the stage. Tennessee Williams was, in fact, forced to rewrite Maxine's entrance to accommodate the thunderous ovation that greeted Davis every evening.

The Night of the Iguana opened on December 28, 1961, and was well-received by the critics. All agreed that it was above-average Williams, and Bette's contribution was praised. The New York *Journal American* observed, "Bette Davis, displaying an unbuttoned shirt, a shock of flame-colored hair and the most raucously derisive laugh this side of a fish wharf, is marvelously brash and beguiling." For The New York *Times*, Walter Kerr wrote, "... in the coarse and blowzy effrontery of her flat-footed walk...there is some tattered and forlorn splendor."

Davis was flattered by her good reviews and the enthusiastic reception she received from audiences, but her resentment toward her co-workers deepened. Reportedly, Williams sided with O'Neal and Leighton against Bette during several heated disputes. By early April, she had left the production and was replaced by Shelley Winters. Davis told a reporter at the time, "I don't want to go on for another six months. I'm going to rest and walk in the country..."

As it turned out, Bette did more than walk during this brief period of relaxation—she also read and re-read a screenplay that had been submitted to her by director Robert Aldrich. The script told the story of a demented former child star from the vaudeville era who torments her sister, a crippled former movie queen, in their decaying Hollywood mansion.

July 19, 1962: Bette, Jack Warner, Joan Crawford and director Robert Aldrich pose in Warner's trophy room at the studio following the announcement that Davis and Crawford will costar for the first time in "an unusual mystery-thriller" entitled *Whatever Happened To Baby Jane?* The production marked Bette's return to the Warner lot after an absence of thirteen years. Crawford (who was considered Davis' chief rival while she was under contract to the studio during the late Forties) had also not worked for Warner for a decade.

The *Baby Jane* screenplay, based on an original story by Henry Farrell, was first discovered by Aldrich, who—at Crawford's urging —had been looking for a vehicle to unite the two actresses for years. He was delighted when both Davis and Crawford agreed to the project, but raising money for the picture turned out to be extremely difficult. Aldrich explained in an interview, "Four major companies declined even to read the script or scan the budget. Three distributors read the script...and turned the project down. Two of these said they might be interested if I would agree to cast younger players." Finally, Aldrich obtained independent financing, with Warner agreeing to distribute the film. The two stars accepted lower-than-usual salaries, but requested percentage points from any profits the film might accrue.

Crawford and Davis chat in a rare moment of inactivity during *Baby Jane* production. The filming schedule—thanks to the tight budget—was highly accelerated. Crawford recalled, "...we had to shoot it so quickly and improvise so many interiors—and even exteriors—I felt as though we were filming a newsreel, not a movie...we shot the film as though there'd be no tomorrow."

Fortunately, Bette and Joan were seasoned pros who had gone through dozens of "quickie" productions over the years, and they both knew instinctively that this film could singlehandedly revive their careers. Consequently, neither star indulged in displays of temperament that might have slowed down filming. In fact, the rapid production pace precluded the full-blown feud that columnists predicted for the volatile, veteran stars. This is not to suggest, however, that there were not touchy moments or an occasional bitchy remark. Joan and Bette were unlike each other in their approach to their careers; Davis was concerned with the challenge of the work, while Joan—though equally professional—was on constant guard to keep her manicured image intact. As filming on *Baby Jane* progressed, the differences between the two stars and their innate sense of competition with each other led to a tense atmosphere on the set, but only an over-zealous publicity department would characterize the situation as a *feud*.

OPPOSITE: When B.D.—who played a small role in the film—saw Bette in makeup as Baby Jane Hudson for the first time, she shook her head in disbelief and said, "This time, mother, you've finally gone too far." Indeed, Davis' well-known penchant for authenticity had never been so unflatteringly realized. She told Whitney Stine, "Jane's appearance, I felt, was fascinating—and just exactly the way she would look. I felt Jane never washed her face, just added another layer of makeup each day."

Davis also insisted that she be photographed harshly, and requested Ernest Haller to shoot the film. Ironically, Haller had worked on almost a dozen of Bette's past films because she felt he took such care to flatter her. When *Baby Jane* was released, critics applauded the courage it took for Bette to allow herself to appear so grotesque on screen. One review compared her mouth to a greasy bow tie that had slipped up over her chin. Several months later, however, Davis had second thoughts about her appearance in the picture. During a screening at the Cannes Film Festival, she turned to Aldrich with tears in her eyes and said, "I look awful. Do I really look that awful?"

RIGHT: Director Aldrich—prone on the sand in pointy hat—oversees a rehearsal of one of the final scenes of *Baby Jane*. By this time, Davis and Crawford were exhausted and irritable. Although Aldrich remembers, "They behaved absolutely perfectly. They never allowed an abrasive word to slip out. They didn't try to upstage each other," there can be no doubt that there was a great deal of animosity just below the surface. Crawford told one writer, "Bette, in an interview, referred to me as a 'movie star' and to herself as an 'actress.' I still wonder what the hell had she become if not a movie star? With all her little gestures with the cigarette, the clipped speech, the big eyes...I was just as much an actress as she was."

More than her acting abilities, it was Crawford's pretentions that Bette resented. She called her Joan of Crawford and made fun of her studied grandeur, referring to Joan as "bless you," an expression Crawford constantly used in place of a simple "thank you." In turn, Joan was shocked at Bette's lack of interest in glamour, and made several comments about the robe and slippers that Davis favored off camera. On a deeper level, Crawford must surely have felt envious of the fact that Davis had the juicier role in the film, while Bette probably felt a tinge of jealousy every time she looked at Joan's still-magnificent face and remembered the glossy production values that MGM had lavished on Crawford's vehicles at a time when Davis had to scratch and claw for the slightest perk from Warner.

OPPOSITE: For publicity photographs, Davis and Julie Allred act out "I've Written A Letter To Daddy," a song they both perform in the film; Allred as young Jane, vaudeville headliner, and Bette as the middle-aged, mentally-deteriorating Jane—who plans on using the song in an ill-conceived comeback.

Situation Wanted, Women 98
Artists

MOTHER OF THREE - 10, 11 & 15 - DIVORCÉE. AMERICAN. THIRTY YEARS EXPERIENCE AS AN ACTRESS IN MOTION PICTURES. MOBILE STILL AND MORE AFFABLE THAN RUMOR WOULD HAVE IT. WANTS STEADY EMPLOYMENT IN HOLLYWOOD. (HAS HAD BROADWAY.)
Bette Davis, c/o Martin Baum, G.A.C.
REFERENCES UPON REQUEST.

ABOVE: Less than two weeks after completing *Baby Jane*, Davis ran this ad in *The Hollywood Reporter*, a film industry trade publication. The reaction was immediate: Hollywood was stunned. It looked as though one of the movies' greatest stars was begging desperately for work. Bette later confessed that the ad was "half playful and half serious." Playful because Davis was hardly down and out. Advance word on *Baby Jane* indicated a smash hit, and Bette's autobiography, *The Lonely Life*, had been released to fine reviews and strong sales all over the country. The serious side of the *Reporter* ad was simply Davis—in a sardonic mood—informing studios and producers that she was back in town and eager for more work.

RIGHT: The advertising campaign for *Baby Jane* left little doubt that the picture was not the usual Davis or Crawford fare. The "thriller" element of the film was exploited to appeal to the vast teenage movie-going population, while older fans of the two stars were warned to expect the unexpected. The movie opened in October 1962, and instantly became the year's surprise box-office bonanza, earning back its production costs in just eleven days.

Whatever Happened To Baby Jane? received mixed critical notices. Some reviewers responded negatively to the sensational, horrific aspects of the picture, which many felt were unworthy of the stature of its stars. Typical of this attitude was Bosley Crowther's review in the New York *Times*: "Joan Crawford and Bette Davis make a couple of formidable freaks...But we're afraid this unique conjunction of two one-time top-ranking stars in a story about two aging sisters who were once theatrical celebrities themselves does not afford either opportunity to do more than wear grotesque costumes, make up to look like witches and chew the scenery to shreds." The New York *Herald Tribune* review, however, complimented the performances: "If Miss Davis' portrait of an outrageous slattern with the mind of an infant has something of the force of a hurricane, Miss Crawford's performance as the crippled sister could be described as the eye of that hurricane. Both women are seen in the isolated decay of two spirits left to dry on the desert by the receding flood of fame. 'I didn't bring your breakfast because you didn't eat your din-din,' Miss Davis tells Miss Crawford. She then howls a witch's laugh that would frizzle the mane of a wild beast. It is the mingling of baby-talk and baby-mindedness with the behavior of an ingenious gauleiter that raises the hackles."

Baby Jane succeeded with audiences and most critics because the talented people involved approached their work with a seriousness and dedication that belied the exploitative, horror angle of the screenplay. It seems safe to assume that the film would not have endured as a popular classic if it had been made by a lesser cast or director. Seen today, *Baby Jane* remains an effective thriller and an acting tour-de-force for its stars. Some scenes now have a camp quality because of their familiarity; and the moments in which Davis physically abuses Crawford have taken on new meaning since the revelations in *Mommie Dearest*.

For the first time in years, Davis agreed to make personal appearances to promote *Baby Jane*. She even travelled in a studio-supplied, decorated bus to several theaters in the New York City area to greet audiences who waited hours to see her. Here, Bette is joined on stage by B.D., who is holding a doll used in a give-away promotion on behalf of the picture.

Davis also appeared on several TV shows to drum up interest in *Baby Jane*, and she often related how difficult it had been to raise the money to produce the film. She told of the numerous turn-downs from producers who were unwilling to make a picture with "those two old broads." Audiences loved Bette's candor, but Joan Crawford was not amused. She sent Davis a message requesting that she refrain in the future from referring to her in that manner. In a further promotion move, Davis recorded a "Twist beat" song entitled *Whatever Happened To Baby Jane?* that was not in the film, but received airplay on radio stations across the country. This 45-rpm record has become a prized collector's item.

OPPOSITE: Bette is all smiles at the close of 1962, which had turned out to be her most successful year in over a decade. *Baby Jane* suddenly thrust Davis back onto the list of the most bankable movie performers, and as a result she was once again receiving major scripts. Overnight, she was back in the spotlight reserved only for the most accomplished and successful of celebrities. There was even talk of another Oscar for her *Baby Jane* performance. It was a remarkable Hollywood comeback story, especially for an actress over fifty in the increasingly youth-oriented film industry.

RIGHT: On the December 20, 1962 Andy Williams television show, Davis performs a song resurrected from *Two's Company* entitled "Just Turn Me Loose." It was an appropriate title symbolizing Bette's hard-earned new spirit and the end of her "ten black years."

BELOW: Davis began 1963 with an unusual TV assignment. When Raymond Burr became ill, the producers of his highly-rated series *Perry Mason* decided to utilize guest stars in *Mason*-like stories rather than try to find another actor to replace Burr in the show. Bette starred as a savvy criminal lawyer in "The Case of Constant Doyle," and her appearance won the episode high ratings.

OPPOSITE: Bette and Patty Duke beam proudly after receiving Gold Medal Awards from *Photoplay* magazine during March 1963 ceremonies in Hollywood. Davis was named the 1962 Actress of the Year for her *Baby Jane* performance; Duke accepted the Best Picture award for *The Miracle Worker*, in which she costarred.

As predicted, Bette received her

first Oscar nomination in years for *Baby Jane*; surprisingly, Crawford was passed over. Not to be upstaged, however, Joan agreed to accept for the odds-on favorite to win as Best Actress, Anne Bancroft in *The Miracle Worker*. When the winner was announced, Bette was chagrined to see Joan Crawford receive a thunderous ovation from the crowd moments after the Oscar had gone to Bancroft.

TOP LEFT: Robert Aldrich and Bette attend another Hollywood function, shortly after it was announced that they planned to work together again on a follow-up to *Baby Jane* entitled *Hush. . . Hush, Sweet Charlotte*, which would reunite Davis and Crawford. First, though, Bette had a movie to make for Jack Warner: a murder mystery entitled *Dead Pigeon*, in which she would play twins.

BOTTOM LEFT: By the time filming had begun on *Dead Pigeon*, the title had been changed to the more appropriate *Dead Ringer*. Based on an earlier Dolores Del Rio vehicle, the film's storyline focussed on the revenge murder of a callous wealthy woman by her twin sister, who is barely getting by as the owner of a downtown Los Angeles bar. As in *A Stolen Life*, the more sympathetic of the two sisters assumes the identity of the dead twin (pictured), but in this film the consequences are tragic.

Dead Ringer, while less sensational than *Baby Jane*, was nonetheless a box-office winner for Bette, who was now being referred to as a "Horror Queen." Reviews were mixed, but most critics agreed that having Davis back in a full-fledged star turn was worth the price of admission. The New York *Times* reflected, "Remember that celebrated Warner Bros. ad a few years ago that proudly claimed, 'Nobody's as good as Bette when she's bad'? Well, Bette Davis is back and she is very, very bad. Her mammoth creation of a pair of murderous twin sisters not only galvanizes this uncommonly silly little film, but it is great fun to watch."

Paul Henreid was hired to direct
Dead Ringer, and he and Bette oblig-
ingly recreated the legendary cigarette scene from *Now, Voyager*
for news photographers. Henreid
framed the *Dead Ringer* proceedings
within the style of a Forties melodrama, and he handled the scenes of
mayhem well. Particularly effective
is a vicious attack by an enormous
Great Dane on the dead sister's
lover, played by Peter Lawford. The
scenes of Bette playing both twins
on screen were also quite convincing. She remembers, "Paul and I
worked very hard to make it plau-
sible at all...It was even better
thought out than the split screen in
A Stolen Life, plus Connie Cezon was
such an unbelievable double for me
—we could actually use her in some
of the scenes."

A playful moment from Bette's second 1964 release, *The Empty Canvas*, in which she played the glamorous, wealthy mother of Horst Bucholz, seen here. Produced in Rome by Carlo Ponti, the film appealed to Davis initially because she was told that her role would be enlarged once production began. When it wasn't, Bette decided to make her character more noticeable by affecting a Texas accent and wearing a blond dutch-boy hairstyle.

As a result of these efforts, Davis emerged as the most interesting element of the picture, but *The Empty Canvas* never found an audience. It was Bette's first failure since her comeback, and she realized that she would have to choose her roles more carefully if she was going to maintain the renewed momentum of her career.

OPPOSITE: Davis and Susan Hayward eye each other with suspicion –and pose with forced cordiality–at the press party announcing the start of production on *Where Love Has Gone*. Bette signed to portray Susan's mother in the film, based on Harold Robbins' steamy best-seller, a thinly-disguised fictionalization of the murder of Lana Turner's lover by her teenage daughter which had dominated newspaper headlines six years earlier.

Bette has admitted that she took this one-dimensional role (in what she knew would be a trashy soap opera) in order to pay for a lavish Beverly Hills wedding for B.D.– who, at sixteen, had decided to marry a young film company executive. "It was the hardest thing I ever did," Davis recalls, "giving my permission for B.D. to marry...I didn't want to lose her so early in her life. But...I believed she was mature enough at sixteen to know her own mind. In many ways she was ninety." Bette created a stir by giving her daughter away in the ceremony, something that is allowed in the Episcopal Church.

The *Where Love Has Gone* script
allowed for very little shading in the
performances of the cast. At one
point, in the midst of a loud argument, Davis accuses Hayward of
sleeping around with a variety of unworthy men. Hayward responds,
"When you're dying of thirst, you'll
drink from a mudhole!"

The atmosphere on the *Where
Love Has Gone* set was, to quote a
line from *All About Eve*, "very
Macbeth-ish." Hayward, who had
been labeled "a bargain-basement
Bette Davis," was nervous and insecure about working with Bette.
The film's director, Edward
Dmtryk, recalled, "Actually, Susan
was scared to death of Bette. Susan
was a very difficult person to know.
She was very reserved, nervous and
withdrawn. Bette mistook that, ap-
parently, for rudeness. They were
exact opposites." At one point things
got so tense that Bette threw her
grey wig at Hayward and asked if
she wanted to play both roles.

OPPOSITE: Davis gestures toward a
portrait of her character that became
the center of a major dispute after
principal photography on the picture
had been completed. Paramount
wanted Bette to return to the studio
to shoot a brief scene in which she
suddenly, inexplicably goes insane,
slashing her portrait. Davis flatly refused to even consider the idea, and
despite legal threats, she held her
ground. In place of Bette's tacked-on
insanity, it was decided that Hayward would go berserk and destroy
the painting prior to committing
suicide.

Where Love Has Gone received predictable reviews. *Time* called the picture "...a few innings of big-league
smut scraped together from the
novel by Harold Robbins." Bette,
however, emerged unscathed. *News-
week* said of her, "Bette Davis
is splendid, with her eyes rolling
and her mouth working and her in-
credible lines to say. Sitting in the
ugliest chair in Hollywood, she
lowers her teacup and pronounces:
'Somewhere along the line the world
has lost all its standards and all its
taste.'" Despite its trashiness—or
because of it—the movie was a box-
office winner.

LEFT: A rare candid photo of Bette and her daughter Margot. From the time it became obvious that Margot had to be kept in special schools, Davis made sure—no matter what her schedule—that Margot spent her summers and holidays at home with her family. In a 1979 interview, Bette sadly admitted that Margot's mental age remains approximately six or seven.

BELOW: At a Hollywood Christmas gala in December 1964, Bette helps remove Richard Chamberlain's makeup following his performance as Santa Claus.

An early script reading on the Twentieth Century-Fox set of *Hush...
Hush, Sweet Charlotte*, with Joseph Cotten, Bette, Robert Aldrich and Joan Crawford. The disparity between the personalities of Davis and Crawford is clear: Bette is all business, studying her script with her glasses perched on her nose, wearing a simple hairdo. Joan is every inch the star–dressed elegantly, wearing an elaborate hairstyle and flashy jewelry; a Pepsi-Cola bottle (Crawford was an executive with the soft drink company) is prominent. She is very much aware that there is a photographer present.

Shortly after production on *Charlotte* began, Crawford became ill with a respiratory infection serious enough for her to be hospitalized.

Aldrich tried to keep the filming on schedule by shooting around Joan, concentrating on Bette's scenes. Crawford returned to the studio, but she was still not well enough to work, and after a few sluggish days she re-entered the hospital. It became clear that she would have to be replaced, and several veteran stars were considered, including Katharine Hepburn and Vivien Leigh. The response Fox received from Leigh was astonishingly rude: "I could just about look at Joan Crawford's face in a southern plantation at seven o'clock in the morning," she said, "but I couldn't possibly look at Bette Davis'!" Finally, Bette's good friend Olivia de Havilland was coaxed from her Paris home to play Charlotte's malevolent cousin Miriam.

TOP LEFT: Bette is demure as she models a *Charlotte* costume designed by Norma Koch, who won an Oscar for her *Baby Jane* wardrobe. The film has been described as a "blood relative" of *Jane.* It was written by that movie's author, Henry Farrell, specifically as a follow-up to the earlier film, and many of the same technical personnel worked on both projects. Initially, Fox executives wanted to name the film *Whatever Happened to Cousin Charlotte?*, but Davis protested that it was too exploitive, and eventually everyone agreed on the final title.

Like *Jane,* this film tells the dark story of a middle-aged woman (Bette) who lives as a recluse—in this instance because of a ghastly decapitation murder in her youth that she feels some responsibility for. She is prone to paranoia and hallucinations about the night of the murder, and her condition is helped along by her cousin (de Havilland) and the cousin's lover, played by Joseph Cotten. Eventually, Charlotte learns that she had nothing to do with the murder—but only after she has done away with de Havilland and Cotten. It is revealed that the axe-wielding murderess of the past is a jealous rival of *Charlotte's* played by another long-time pal of Bette's—Mary Astor, in her final acting assignment.

BOTTOM LEFT: Davis and de Havilland consume a Chinese meal with gusto following a long day of *Charlotte* filming. Bette was delighted to be working with her old Warner buddy again, and she was relieved that the Crawford situation was over. There was some speculation at the time that Joan's illness was exacerbated by a concentrated effort on the part of Bette and costar Agnes Moorehead to sabotage Crawford's participation on the picture. Davis has always denied that she or anyone else made Joan's life miserable during the few weeks that she was on the production, but there is no denying that the studio's handling of Crawford's dismissal was tactless; she first heard about it over the radio as she lie in the hospital. Her only comment to the press was, "I'm glad for Olivia—she needs a good part."

On the Louisiana location, Bette enjoys a break, out of costume, during *Charlotte* filming. Her performance in the picture proved to be more complex than her work in *Baby Jane*. The levels of her character's mental state were more thoroughly written, and she was able to bring great variety and nuance to the role. *Baby Jane* remains a tighter, more satisfying picture, but Davis' performances in both films serve as fascinating bookends for her reign as "Hollywood's grande-dame ghoul." *Charlotte* was another big moneymaker, and its title song, sung by Patti Page, became an unexpected hit.

Betty and young William Dix in a scene from *The Nanny*, which was filmed in England during the summer of 1965. During production, Davis became friendly with costar Jill Bennett, who told Charles Higham that she admired Bette despite her eccentricities. "She was real, gutsy and *very dangerous*," Bennett said. "Dangerous the way a star should be! And she told me

something wonderful: 'Always make love to your props. To the furniture.' I told her I remembered that moment in *Little Foxes* when she leaned against the door as though she wanted to kiss it. I often found myself making love to tea trays in pictures after that." Bennett also recalled an excursion to the horseraces when Bette was dressed to kill and (because Bennett had worn a simple dress), Davis insisted that she follow behind her like a secretary–which Bennett, amused at the situation, did gladly.

While working on *The Nanny*, Davis received word that her long battle with Gary Merrill over visitation rights for their son had been settled. A judge decided that Gary would be able to see Michael on weekends and on certain holidays pending Bette's approval. Davis took the decision gracefully and told Bennett that her feelings for Merrill had softened–and that she often recalled, with nostalgia, the early happy years of their union.

OPPOSITE: Critic Judith Crist, in the New York *Herald Tribune*, called Bette's performance as *The Nanny*, "a beautifully-controlled performance as a jealous and voracious nursemaid pitted against a willful and obviously disturbed 10-year-old (Dix)." While not strictly a thriller, *The Nanny* contained enough spooky scenes (the drowning of a child, a woman dying horribly because she is unable to get to her medication) that it appealed to the audiences that had supported Bette's recent forays into the macabre. It was, however, not as financially successful as her last few films.

Following *The Nanny*, Davis took a year-and-a-half off from movie making. She moved from Los Angeles back to New England–this time to Westport, Connecticut–and she appeared occasionally on television, once with Milton Berle in a skit entitled *The Maltese Chicken*. She also considered several submitted scripts. She was personally approached by Jacqueline Susann to play Helen Lawson in *Valley of the Dolls*, a role that went to Judy Garland, who was eventually replaced by Susan Hayward. She also discussed starring, as a lesbian, in the controversial British film *The Killing of Sister George*, but the part was taken by Beryl Reid. In 1967, Bette returned to England to film a play about the domineering mother of all time, *The Anniversary*.

As Mrs. Taggart in this closeup from *The Anniversary*, Bette brings to mind a glamorous, knife-swinging pirate. Actually, her character was a manipulative shrew who brings her odd assortment of three sons—one is a transvestite, one is henpecked and the other is a womanizer—together each year to celebrate the anniversary of her marriage to their father, who has been dead for a decade. The script, by *Nanny* screenwriter Jimmy Sangster, was never polished to Bette's satisfaction and she found herself at odds with director Alvin Rakoff and several members of the cast.

Costar Sheila Hancock had never worked with a star of Davis' stature, and she said in an interview, "I was shocked when (Sangster) gave a lecture saying that Miss Davis liked to be treated with great adulation." She recalled a scene in which Bette had to do several takes on a staircase, and the crew burst into applause after even the dullest take. Davis is, to be sure, expectant of respectful treatment, but if she was indeed indulging in prima donna behavior during this production, it probably had to do with her unhappiness with the entire project. Working with the eyepatches required for her role made her extremely uncomfortable. Much worse, she wasn't receiving the guidance she needed for the physical business involved in a scene. "At the end of a take, it's very dark," she said. "I want to know what's going on. I ask 'Haven't I hit my mark?...Haven't I hit a light? Have I covered somebody in a shot?' Nobody answers me. I just hear this terrible whispering, and a voice shouts 'Let's have another take.' I ask 'Why?' and the answer is, 'Just let's have another take.'"

Rakoff was soon fired and Roy Ward Baker, whom Bette knew and trusted, was brought in to complete the picture. Conditions were not greatly improved, however, with Baker at the helm. Sheila Hancock claimed that Bette once said, "I hate a good atmosphere on a picture... any film that had been miserable to make was a success."

Unfortunately, that axiom proved untrue in the case of *The Anniversary*. Released in the first months of 1968, the movie was met with critical scorn and public indifference. To promote the film, Davis appeared on the *Tonight Show*—and appropriately brought an eyepatch with her for Johnny Carson, who was suffering an eye disorder at the time. *The Anniversary* was not a good picture, but it at least marked the end of Bette's horror cycle, which had certainly outlived its usefulness.

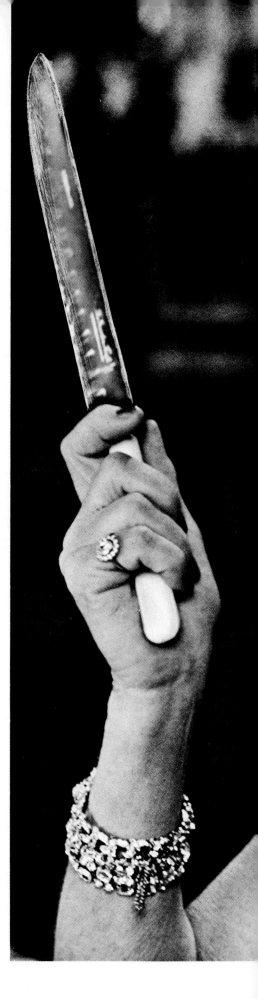

OPPOSITE: Within a few months, Bette was back in England to film *Connecting Rooms*, in which she played a cellist who performs on the street to support her modest lifestyle. The picture is a character study about a diverse group of people who reside in a rundown boarding house. Costarred with Davis was Sir Michael Redgrave as an ex-professor who has lost his job because he is homosexual. There is also a young rock musician thrown in for generation-gap complications. Bette and Sir Michael—who had agreed to the project so that they could work together—discovered too late that they both felt the script was terrible.

The production utilized several public locations (such as the one pictured), and Bette was both flattered and annoyed by the swarms of people who turned up at every location to see her. One evening shoot had to be delayed for hours until the crowd could be controlled. Upon completion, *Connecting Rooms* was considered so poor that it received scant distribution. Most Davis fans in the United States have never seen the film.

RIGHT: After returning from England, Bette appeared in an episode of Robert Wagner's TV series, *To Catch A Thief*. She was cast as a safecracker in the show, titled "A Touch of Magic." The role afforded Davis another opportunity to adopt several different guises; a dilapidated convalescent, a chic matron (pictured) and a wisecracking nun. Bette accepted the part primarily because of Wagner, who had over the years become a dear friend. Davis was thrilled when he remarried Natalie Wood (Bette's "daughter" in *The Star*) two years later.

BELOW: Bette joins producer Mervyn LeRoy, Edward G. Robinson, Jack Warner and Rosalind Russell at a lavish soundstage party to salute Warner upon his retirement from film making. In a short speech, Davis told the star-studded audience that she loved Warner as a father, "even when he scolded me!" She also contributed the evening's most poignant moment when she asked for a standing tribute in honor of all of the personalities whom she and Warner had known who had passed on. "The room's so full of people who knew each other so well," she said. "And so few of us are left."

OPPOSITE: A dramatic study of Davis and Zalman King taken during the filming of an episode of TV's *Gunsmoke*. Bette portrayed a feisty widow with four sons in the hour-long show, which was filmed in six days—a schedule she characterized as "cutting it a little close."

As the Sixties ended, Bette looked back on the decade with mixed feelings. Her enormously successful return to the forefront of her profession in *Whatever Happened To Baby Jane?* had proven to be both a blessing and a curse. She was, of course, pleased to be working again with such regularity, but she became typecast in the horror genre for several years, and she was relieved that period seemed to be over.

By 1969, Bette's personal life had become more tranquil. B.D.'s marriage had turned out to be lasting; she and her husband owned a New England farm and they had made Bette a grandmother. Michael was now in college studying law, and Bette found quiet contentment in her Connecticut home—far away from Hollywood. She was more financially secure than she had been a decade earlier, and she enjoyed being in a position where she could return to work when she chose to.

THE
SEVENTIES
AND
EIGHTIES

RIGHT: Bette begins the Seventies with a tip of her hat—a straw hat awarded to her by Fabergé in New York at a February 1970 gala celebrating her enduring career. Unfortunately, the film Davis was considering doing next would add little luster to her reputation. Entitled *Bunny and Billy*, it concerned a middle-aged couple who, because of various circumstances, decide to team up and rob banks—dressed as hippies. By October, Bette had signed for the picture and was back in Hollywood for costume tests. She was optimistic about the project, and was delighted when Ernest Borgnine agreed to costar.

BOTTOM RIGHT: Borgnine and Davis in costume and on location in Albuquerque, New Mexico for *Bunny O'Hare*, the film's final title. Although stunt people were used for long shots of the couple speeding away from their robberies on motorcycle, Bette recalls that doubles were not always satisfactory for director Gerald Oswald: "There is no reason why Borgnine and I weren't killed," she said, "in some of the shots up and down those New Mexico mountain roads."

Bunny O'Hare turned out to be a botched off-beat comedy in its released form. American International Pictures disliked Oswald's final cut and it was re-edited by the studio. Bette considered this version a far cry from the picture she had made, and she instigated legal action against AIP. Eventually, the suit was dropped, but the resultant publicity did little to encourage strong box-office grosses. Bette's eightieth movie was not a hit, and it is doubtful that even the original version would have succeeded. Critics did cheer Bette's versatility, and comment was made about some of her dialogue. During her first attempt at bank robbery, Bunny says to the teller, "I've got a gun in my purse. How would you like your guts spilled all over this floor?" The line, as delivered in Davis' clipped speech pattern, always gets a laugh. Her final line raised some eyebrows: exasperated by her ungrateful grown children—for whom she has been robbing banks—Bunny is asked by Borgnine what they will think if he and Bunny run off together. "Fuck 'em!" she shouts.

OPPOSITE: Early in 1972, Bette travelled to England to star with Robert Wagner in *Madame Sin*, a James Bond-type adventure that was shown as a TV series pilot in the U.S. and in theaters in Europe. In the title role, Davis had one of her most unusual parts as a witchy, half-Chinese, power-mad woman who lives in a Scottish castle loaded with typical spy-movie gadgetry. She is an unremittingly evil character, and at one point Wagner says to her, "You're not a woman, you're a disease!"

Madame Sin is an amusing spy spoof, but it came along just a few years too late to capitalize on the public's fascination with Bond-like pictures, despite an ad campaign that claimed, "Even the diabolical *Dr. No* would have to say yes to *Madame Sin*."

During pre-production on the picture in Hollywood, Davis was surprised by Ralph Edwards for his *This Is Your Life* TV show (with the help of Wagner and designer Edith Head). Guests who paid tribute to Bette included her sister Bobby, William Wyler, Olivia de Havilland and *Baby Jane* costar Victor Buono.

Davis responded to the surprise in typical fashion: "I was in a state of complete shock. Told both Wagner and Head I was going to murder them!"

Upon Bette's return from *Madame Sin* locations, she filmed another TV movie/pilot entitled *The Judge and Jake Wyler*, in which she was cast as a retired judge who fights crime with the aid of a young parolee, played by Doug McClure. Neither *Jake Wyler* nor *Madame Sin* were picked up as series. Also in 1972, Davis appeared in a cameo role in an Italian production, *The Scientific Cardplayer*, for producer Dino de Laurentiis. The film, which starred Alberto Sordi, was a hit in Italy, but was barely distributed in the United States.

ABOVE: Summer 1972: Bette seems stunned by the loud welcome she is given by an enthusiastic crowd—and Lana Turner—as she is introduced at a lavish celebration of the 1940s held at New York's Roseland ballroom. The evening was a nostalgia orgy for movie fans, who got to meet —and pay tribute to—such stars as Jane Russell, June Allyson, Jane Withers and Van Johnson.

RIGHT: Bette and Jimmy Stewart stroll on the MGM lot, where they were both filming separate projects: Stewart was starring in a short-lived series, while Davis was working on another pilot, *Hello Mother, Goodbye*. The pilot didn't lead to a series, but Bette was happy just to have had lunch with Stewart at the studio, "I told Jimmy I had waited forty years for a date with him. One must never give up one's dreams! They do come true." It was, however, another decade before Davis and Stewart worked together for the first time.

BOTTOM: May 14, 1973: Anne Baxter congratulates Bette after presenting her with the Sarah Siddons Award at a Chicago ceremony. The Margo Channing/Eve Harrington relationship had now come full circle. The Sarah Siddons Award was a fictitious honor dreamed up for *All About Eve*. In the film, Eve wins the award in a role that Margo was originally set to do. Years later, a Chicago group created the award in honor of the movie—even down to duplicating the trophy exactly. When Bette/Margo was named as the 1973 recipient, who better than Anne/Eve to present it to her? Coincidentally, Bette would soon be returning to Margo's domain: the theater.

OPPOSITE: For once, Bette stars in a TV movie not intended to lead to a series: *Scream, Pretty Peggy*, broadcast on the ABC network in November, 1973. Davis played the terrorized mother of Ted (*That Girl*) Bessell, who turns out to be a pathological transvestite! Even the title of this sordid project smacked of Bette's *Baby Jane* period.

RIGHT: Davis takes center stage in Boston as part of a sporadic one-woman stage tour she took to colleges and auditoriums across the country during the mid-Seventies. The evening began with a series of clips from Bette's films. She then appeared on stage to answer questions from the audience. In response to the inevitable query about Joan Crawford, Bette said diplomatically, "I never feuded with Joan. We didn't have time, and besides we were much too professional for such nonsense...she was a fine actress."

A highlight of the evening was her tip on how to do a Davis impression: "You flail your arms all about, while rolling your hips, take a big drag from the cigarette and say, 'Peter ...the letter.'" Bette added that she could never figure out why the name Peter is always used—since she never said that name on screen.

RIGHT: Barry Manilow, Bette and Dick Cavett enjoy a laugh on Cavett's show, aired in 1974. Davis told an amusing story about her earliest days in Hollywood: "They didn't know what to do with something that looked like me. At that age, I want to tell you, in 1930, I was the *Yankee-est*, most modest virgin who ever walked the earth! They laid me on a couch, and I tested fifteen men." The audience roared, even as Bette explained that she meant *screen* tested.

OPPOSITE: Rare advertising art for *Miss Moffat*, the musical based on *The Corn Is Green* which was to mark Bette's return to Broadway in 1974. Writer/Director Joshua Logan approached Davis about the project after Mary Martin decided against it. Bette was receptive despite her misgivings about returning to the stage. She liked the prospect of playing Miss Moffat again, especially now that her age was closer to the character's, and she was impressed with Logan's decision to relocate the story from a Welsh mining town to a small black village in the south. She was also reassured that the show's score would be modified to accommodate her limited vocal abilities.

Although she was confident at first, once rehearsals began Davis suffered serious anxiety about carrying a large-scale musical into New York. She did not relate well to Dorian Harewood, her young costar, and she confided to Logan that she felt she might not possess enough vocal strength to project the dialogue, much less sing. By the time *Miss Moffat* opened in Philadelphia, Davis was a nervous wreck –and she felt little joy that advance ticket sales in New York had already guaranteed a six-month run for the show.

During one Philadelphia performance, to Logan's horror, Bette turned to the audience and said, "How can I play this scene?" She had fouled up a cue for Harewood and thought the goof was his fault. When she realized her error, she turned again to the audience and said, "I was wrong. I want you to know that. It wasn't his fault. Go back, Dorian, and we'll start over." A mortified Harewood did what he was told, muttering under his breath. The audience loved it, but Logan's stomach was churning–and he knew at that moment that the show was doomed.

As Bette became more and more uncomfortable with the whole enterprise, her nerves gave way to illness. She suffered from chronic sore throats, and after one matinee she collapsed in severe pain from her old back injury. Logan was advised by her doctor that if she continued with the production she would face grave physical consequences–she was, after all, over sixty-five years old. Davis left the show, and–confined

to a wheelchair–returned to Connecticut to recover. Logan, who was near collapse himself, was convinced that Bette exaggerated her illness to get out from under her obligations. But by all accounts, she was genuinely distressed at having to back out of *Miss Moffat*–although she was certainly relieved to have the ordeal over with.

ABOVE: Still in a wheelchair, Bette attends a gala at the Hollywood Palladium. After taking most of 1975 off, her health had improved considerably, and she decided to sign for her first major movie in five years, *Burnt Offerings*.

190

OPPOSITE: Costar Karen Black eyes Davis with wary admiration on the set of *Burnt Offerings*. Davis played the aunt of Oliver Reed in this clichéd tale of a large old house that exerts unexplainable power over a family living there for the summer. Originally to have been directed by Bob Fosse seven years earlier, it was produced, directed and co-written by Dan Curtis for August 1976 release by United Artists.

Bette was not pleased with the production of *Burnt Offerings*. She told one interviewer that she was "appalled by the lack of discipline in current film making...there's practically no rehearsal, and the sloppy attitude on the set is unbelievable. These people that have been bred on television production have no sense of pacing or style...it's all 'just get it in the can.'" She also found little to like about her costars. Oliver Reed professed to be "in awe" of Bette—but mostly, it seems, he was just hungover. Davis also had difficulty relating to Karen Black's open-ended, improvisational approach to acting, and she was grateful when filming ended. *Burnt Offerings* was not a moneymaker, and critics disliked it. *Variety* characterized it as "a talky supernatural picture." And of Bette, the paper noted, "Unkind lighting and costuming make her resemble Baby Jane Hudson; it's a shame to see her in a film like this."

ABOVE RIGHT: Bette fared much better in her next TV movie, *The Disappearance of Aimee*, in which she costarred with Faye Dunaway. Aired on November 16, 1976 over NBC as the twenty-fifth anniversary presentation of the "Hallmark Hall of Fame," this excellent drama concerned the mysterious month-long disappearance from Los Angeles of radio evangelist Aimee Semple McPherson in 1926. When McPherson (Dunaway) returns, she tells a horrifying story of being brutally kidnapped, but witnesses come forth to swear that she was actually keeping house in a rented bungalow with a married man during her absence. The crux of the screenplay is the trial that is held to determine the truth, and how McPherson and her no-nonsense mother (Davis) manipulate the jury and the public into siding with the charismatic preacher.

Director Anthony Harvey (*The Lion in Winter*) clearly intimates in his film that McPherson is lying about the kidnapping, but he obscures certain details in such a way as to leave reason for doubt. *The Disappearance of Aimee* was beautifully acted and produced, and it found favor with the critics and the viewing public. The Los Angeles *Times* noted, "Bette Davis summons her familiar crisp authority as a dominating mother who, believing her daughter having met foul play, is full of skepticism and demands for the truth." Bette is particularly effective in a scene in which she takes to Aimee's pulpit to announce that she believes her daughter has been murdered. She builds the monologue with a controlled fervor that is little short of mesmerizing.

During *Aimee* production, Dunaway spoke of Davis to a *Time* magazine writer: "We're kind of alike, and I think something is really there between us." Bette in turn let it be known that she considered Faye to be one of "only a handful of actors today who are genuine movie stars in the classic tradition."

It was mentioned in the *Time* article that Davis had, for many years, tried to put together a film about McPherson for herself, but to no avail. When Dunaway was asked if Bette felt any resentment toward her because she was playing a role Davis had coveted, she responded, "Good God, Bette's been a star since she was seventeen, so she's far beyond that kind of professional jealousy. She has been very generous and kind to me."

On March 1, 1977, Bette was presented with the American Film Institute's Life Achievement Award at a lavish, televised celebration. Here, Davis poses with her award (the first given to a woman) as Jane Fonda—the evening's hostess—and George Stevens, Jr.—president of the AFI—look on. During the course of the evening, Davis was saluted with affection by old friends and colleagues. William Wyler said, "I'm often asked, 'Was she difficult?' I say 'No.' 'Was she easy?' I say 'No.' What I mean is, she *was* difficult, but not in the usually accepted sense. She was difficult in the same way I was difficult. She wanted the best, and to get it, *nothing* was too much trouble. She sometimes wanted more takes on a scene than I did." Olivia de Havilland told the audience that Bette "has had the career I have most envied. . . she got the kind of roles that I always wanted." Natalie Wood related an amusing story about her work in *The Star*, and

Robert Wagner quoted from the script of the *To Catch A Thief* episode he had done with Bette: "Lady, you're beautiful, just beautiful." Henry Fonda, Peter Falk and Geraldine Fitzgerald also sang Davis' praises.

Accepting the prestigious award, Bette said to her audience of admirers, "At the beginning of my career, forty-eight years ago, how could I have possibly imagined that I would be standing here tonight as the recipient of such fabulous compliments for my work. I am truly overcome. This is a treasured evening that will always be in my heart." She also gave Ruthie special credit, calling her "a great champion who worked and slaved for many years to help make (my) dreams come true. How her eyes would have sparkled if she could have been here tonight." Bette closed her remarks by telling the audience, "I'd love to kiss ya, but I just washed ma hair."

OPPOSITE: In January 1978–after an absence of over a year–Bette returned to television in the two-part film *The Dark Secret of Harvest Home*, based on the successful novel by Tom Tryon. Davis played the "Amish-like" matriarch (stoic on the surface, but seemingly kind underneath) of a small picturesque New England village that makes few concessions to contemporary life. In fact, it is discovered that the townspeople practice ancient fertility rites and human sacrifices in order to guarantee an abundant corn crop each season.

This "secret" is discovered by a young couple who settle in the quaint town to escape the rigors of modern-day New York City. Naturally, they become the latest victims of Bette and her clan's weird rituals. At five hours in length, *Harvest Home* became tedious and predictable. Even the film's final "shocking" moments held little suspense or genuine fright. Most critics were unimpressed, although the Los Angeles *Times* did offer, "Everyone in the large cast is terrifically earnest, but in the crunch only Miss Davis, whose ringing authority is as crisp, yet warm, as ever, can snap us back to attention."

Life reflected art a bit while the production was on location in Ohio, which doubled for New England. Bette was harrassed by a local witch's coven who evidently objected to her portrayal. Her dressing room/trailer was pelted with rocks and there were threats that it would be burned down. Davis required local police protection during her stay in the area.

ABOVE: Two wine glasses levitate in mid-air thanks to the telepathic powers of Ike Eisenmann (center) while Bette and Christopher Lee look on in this scene from *Return From Witch Mountain*, Davis' first 1978 release and her first movie for the Disney studios.

As Letha Wedge, Bette helps Lee kidnap Eisenmann to exploit his psychic powers for financial gain. This tame, escapist fare was a sequel to the 1975 hit *Escape From Witch Mountain*, but this outing did not prove to be as popular with audiences. Most critics felt that Davis was overqualified for her part. The *Hollywood Reporter* noted, "(Lee and Davis) both seem to be having fun with their roles, obviously realizing it's no talent stretch." Bette enjoyed working on the Disney lot, where she was treated as film royalty.

The distinguished cast of *Death On The Nile*: David Niven, George Kennedy, Peter Ustinov, Lois Chiles, Simon MacCorkindale, Bette, Jack Warden, Maggie Smith and Angela Lansbury. This Agatha Christie whodunit followed in the footsteps of 1974's popular *Murder on the Orient Express*, and in typical Christie fashion, it concerns a group of travelers (with supposedly nothing in common) who are thrown together because of a nasty murder. Bette was not thrilled with the complicated location filming in hot, dusty Egypt. She told a visiting journalist that it would have been different in Hollywood's Golden Age. "They'd have built the Nile for you and you would never have known the difference. Nowadays, films have become travelogues and actors stuntmen."

OPPOSITE: Davis models one of the elegant period gowns she wears as Mrs. Von Shuyler, the caustic grande dame who gives such a hard time to her secretary/companion played by Maggie Smith in *Death On The Nile*. Of Bette's performance in the film, Pauline Kael wrote, "Bette Davis' timing is off (she seems much too vigorous for her old-dowager clothes), but she uses her distinctive style of vocal emphasis to get her few laugh lines across." The Los Angeles *Times*, however, felt that "Davis captures the essence of the form." Because of sound problems during location filming, some of Bette's lines had to be dubbed later by Davis impersonator Michael Greer!

TOP RIGHT: When *Death On The Nile* opened in New York in late September 1978, all of the city's newspapers were on strike. To publicize the film, Bette appeared at a rally and plugged her new movie by shouting about it through a bullhorn. To counteract the lack of newspaper exposure, Paramount also distributed over 500,000 flyers to promote *Death On The Nile*. In spite of all of these efforts, the picture did not do as well at the box office as the studio had hoped.

BOTTOM RIGHT: Just a month later, Bette agreed to an autograph party at a West Hollywood record store to encourage the sale of an album of songs she had recorded in England two years earlier. Titled *Miss Bette Davis Sings*, the album featured Davis talk-singing her way through several classic ballads, as well as songs associated with her film career –including "They're Either Too Young or Too Old," "I've Written a Letter To Daddy" and "Hush... Hush, Sweet Charlotte."

She also performs "It Can't Be Wrong," a ballad built on the beautiful theme from Max Steiner's score for *Now, Voyager*, a melody that has become Bette's unofficial musical signature. *Miss Bette Davis Sings* is tastefully arranged by Roger Webb and produced by Norman Newell, but there is an underlying melancholy behind most of the performances. This is particularly noticeable on "Life Is A Lonely Thing," "Until It's Time For You To Go," and "Growing Older, Feeling Younger." Davis was extremely proud of her recorded efforts, and she gladly agreed to other autograph parties and appearances on TV talk shows to plug the album.

The 1970s had been an inconsistent period for Bette professionally; failures outnumbered successes. Happily, though, she was able to close the decade with one of her finest pieces of work in years. She and the gifted Gena Rowlands starred in *Strangers: The Story of a Mother and Daughter*, aired over CBS on Mother's Day, May 13, 1979. The sensitive story by Michael deGuzman and the creative direction of Milton Katselas resulted in an acting tour-de-force for both actresses.

Bette is a stubborn, elderly widow who takes too much pride in her steely independence: she pulls her groceries home in a child's red wagon each week rather than depend on the delivery boy. Her neatly-ordered life is suddenly thrown into emotional turmoil with the arrival of her middle-aged daughter, who has come home to die. There has not been one word of communication between these two women during the twenty years that they have been separated.

After several harsh confrontations, mother and daughter come to an understanding of each other's pain and the bitterness their relationship has perversely thrived on. At the story's end, we are left with the feeling that Rowland's death will occur in a tentatively loving atmosphere and that Bette is resigned to losing her daughter for the last time.

In his review of the film for the New York *Times*, John O'Connor praised Rowlands, but perceptively noted that Bette took a while to get into her character's heart and mind: "The performances are as complex as the relationship being explored. Miss Davis is an institution, very much a national treasure. But her thoroughly familiar mannerisms can be a handicap, and they are precisely that in the opening scenes. She is overwhelming in her passionate withdrawals. The performance verges, again and again, on self-parody. Gradually, though, the Davis magic takes hold and the character comes into its own, wielding the special powers that only a superb actress would dare to use

with utter confidence. By the second half of the film, Miss Davis is in firm control, able to twist her audience expertly around by the simple blinking of a tear-filled eye."

Bette was unable to attend a gala screening of *Strangers* in New York that Spring because she had broken two ribs in a fall, and although she was completely recovered by September, she was out of the country when she won an Emmy, as the year's finest dramatic actress, for her performance in *Strangers*.

The January 20, 1980 episode of *60 Minutes* featured a lengthy segment on Bette in which she talked openly with Mike Wallace about her career, her marriages, her children—and her recent decision to return to Hollywood to live permanently. Davis candidly revealed that remaining a virgin until her first marriage at age twenty-six had been a mistake, and that marrying someone only because "you want to sleep with them is ridiculous." She admitted that she had undergone *two* abortions while married to Ham Nelson, and that she did not regret the decision because she probably would have had to give up her budding career to raise her family.

She spoke glowingly of Ruthie, although she did reveal that when Margot's disability was first discovered, Ruthie advised Bette to return her to the adoption agency. B.D. and Michael were also interviewed, and they both agreed that their mother was never "a star at home," and that she was a loving parent who instilled in her children a sense of self confidence, and insisted that they be well mannered. Wallace

talked with Bette's old friend Joan Blondell (in one of her last appearances), who told him that she felt it was a good idea for Davis to be back in Hollywood, "where the work is."

The final moments of Bette's interview were filmed at Forest Lawn memorial park in Los Angeles (pictured). Davis was shown placing flowers on Ruthie's grave and pointing out her reserved space next to her mother. Comment was made about the location of the memorial, which looks down on the Warner Brothers lot.

Bette frankly told Wallace that one of the reasons she decided to return to Hollywood was to be near Forest Lawn so that when the time came, "people won't have to make that long trip across the country with me." The almost morbid tone of this *60 Minutes* piece seemed oddly timed, as Bette was in fine health and was looking forward to several promising acting challenges. Perhaps her mood was a result of just having learned that her sister Bobby was suffering from terminal cancer.

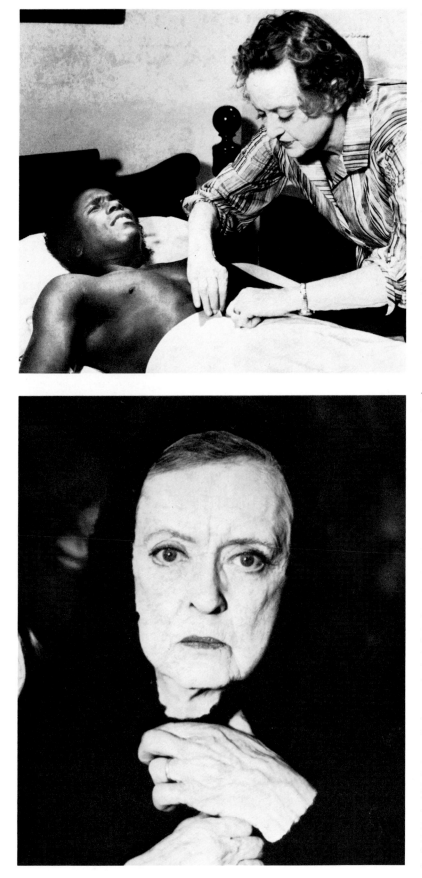

LEFT: *White Mama*, a CBS TV-movie aired March 3, 1980, cast Bette as a penniless widow who is too proud to go on welfare and just a shade too young to collect Social Security benefits. In a desperate move, she takes in a homeless, street-wise black youth (Ernest Harden, Jr.) so that she will receive a monthly stipend for his care.

Inevitably, their vast differences cause the two to clash over matters big and small—not the least of which is her desire for him to pursue his education, while he plans on using his meager boxing ability to fight himself out of the ghetto and away from the woman he derisively calls "White Mama."

When the young man is stabbed in a street fight (pictured), communication between the two breaks down completely. Harden leaves, forcing Davis to become a bag lady, wandering the streets of New York. Eventually they are reunited, with Harden helping Bette to get medical attention. He fights a bloody boxing match in order to win enough money to pay Bette's rent in a condemned building for a year, then joins the Army.

TV Guide touted *White Mama* as "off-beat and heartwarming," but *Variety* called it "A piece of urban whimsy, strictly for people who will believe—or watch—anything." About Davis the paper remarked, "She doesn't sentimentalize the role but, in going so far to the opposite, hard-bitten extreme, she closes out sympathy."

BOTTOM LEFT: During the last months of 1979, Bette had returned to England to star in her second Disney feature, *The Watcher In The Woods*, a suspense thriller about an American family who rent a typically forbidding old house from an elderly recluse (Bette), and soon the young daughters of the family are involved in frightening, bizarre incidents that are finally resolved in a surprise ending complete with startling special effects. Unfortunately, when it opened in May 1980, most critics agreed that *The Watcher In The Woods* was an uneasy mix of Gothic horror and science fiction. After just a week of slow business, Disney pulled the picture and announced that the ending would be re-shot, with the effects beefed up. After a million dollars worth of "improvements," the film was re-released in October 1981—but still the box-office receipts were disappointing.

ABOVE LEFT: Bette's second television movie of the year was aired in November 1980, and afforded her the unusual opportunity to play a gruff ex-stunt pilot. *Skyward* also marked the acting debut of young paraplegic Suzy Gilstrap, playing a wheelchair-bound teenager who yearns to fly—and is able to reach her seemingly impossible goal with the help of veteran pilot Davis. *Skyward* was one of twenty-six-year-old Ron Howard's first major directing assignments, and he was nervous about working with Bette, who called him "Mr. Howard" when they first met. "Please call me Ron," he told her. Davis replied, "I'll call you Mr. Howard until I decide whether I like you or not." Howard was thrilled —and relieved—when, at the end of the first day's shooting, Bette called to him, "Goodnight Ron!"

Skyward was filmed in Texas during an insufferable heat wave, with temperatures often exceeding 110 degrees. Producer Anson Williams was constantly amazed at Bette's stamina and patience. "She never whimpered," he said. "I don't know how she did it. She was in that constant heat for two weeks, all day, every day." When Bette returned from filming, she was often seen wearing a T-shirt emblazoned with "I survived the Texas heat." *Skyward* was well-received critically, and its positive statement about the dreams of the disabled was highly praised. For a TV movie, it received an unusual premiere screening—at the Kennedy Center in Washington, D.C., sponsored by the U.S. Council for the International Year of Disabled Persons.

ABOVE: Singer Kim Carnes joins
Bette in a champagne toast to celebrate the tremendous success of
Carnes' recording "Bette Davis
Eyes" during the Spring of 1981.
The song, written by Jackie De
Shannon and Donna Weiss, tells of a
man-eating vixen very much in the
mold of several Davis heroines of
the Thirties and Forties. Besides her
Davis eyes, the lady in the song has
hair of "Harlow gold" and she's "pure
as New York snow."

"Bette Davis Eyes" brought Kim
Carnes long-sought-after rock fame,
and it went on to win several awards,
including a Grammy as the Best
Song of 1981. Bette was flattered
and surprised by the song. As she
told the press, "Finally I am a hit
with my grandson!"

That same grandson, B.D.'s son J. Ashley Hyman, found himself co-starring with Bette in *Family Reunion*, a four-hour drama telecast on NBC in two parts on April 19 and 20, 1981. Davis plays a newly-retired spinster school teacher in the small New England town of Winfield (which her family established), and which is now being threatened by a powerful conglomerate that intends to destroy part of the town to build a shopping mall. Bette is given an un-limited bus ticket for her retirement, and she decides to travel the country with one of her students (Hyman), visiting various members of the Win-field clan and convincing them to return to their home town in order to fight the mall.

Family Reunion is a sentimental fable that could have been told effi-ciently in half the time. *Variety* cracked, "It's not a family portrait, it's a cattle call!" The film did, how-ever, prove to be a ratings success. J. Ashley was cast because Bette felt he would be ideal to play the boy in the script, and she also sensed in him a desire to become an actor. He was not so sure. "I've enjoyed all of it, really," he said. "I like it, but I don't know if I'm going to go on with it. I like a lot of different things—like horses." When asked how he han-dled his first acting assignment, J. Ashley pointed to his grandmother and said, "She tells me what to do." *Family Reunion* was another project that was filmed as a potential weekly series for Bette, but as completed, it showed little promise for develop-ment into a continuing show.

To promote *Family Reunion*, Davis appeared on *Good Morning America* and told David Hartman of the ob-stacles she faced as a talented, opin-ionated, ambitious woman in the days when it was barely acceptable to be so. She also reiterated her belief that if societal attitudes had been more relaxed in her youth, she would have indulged in affairs rather than follow the traditional route. "I might never have married," she told Hartman, "because there's no ques-tion about it, the big romance of my life, really underneath, was the work I do."

OPPOSITE: A stylish Bette makes an entrance at a Hollywood luncheon. Although she often misses New England, Davis is the first to admit that she enjoys the electricity and commotion that her presence always

generates at social functions and film industry events in Los Angeles. Joan Blondell had been right when she told Mike Wallace that being back in the center of the film capital would be therapeutic for Davis; she had more offers for work than she could accept, a beautiful West Hollywood townhouse, and she was surrounded by friends of many years' standing. When the demands of being Holly-wood's unofficial First Lady became too much, she would hop on a plane to visit family and friends on the east coast.

207

OPPOSITE: For her fourth TV movie in as many years, Davis starred in *A Piano For Mrs. Cimino*, a sensitive study about the ignorance and confusion surrounding the condition of senility. Bette is a retired music teacher whose mental faculties have deteriorated to such a degree that her two sons have her declared incompetent to handle her financial affairs. At the competency hearing, they tell officials that their mother has delusions about being spirited away to Argentina. Sure enough, when she is asked who the president is, she replies with confidence, "Juan Peron."

Esther Cimino is promptly confined to a hospital, where her condition is seen as hopeless. Fortunately, she has a caring granddaughter who manages to get Esther transferred to a less expensive convalescent home, where she soon shows marked improvement—she even carries on a flirtation with a clarinet player, played by Keenan Wynn.

Bette's performance in *A Piano For Mrs. Cimino* ranks with some of her finest screen work. She brings a proper mix of vagueness and determination to a character that, played by a lesser talent, might have come off as simply pathetic. *Variety* noted, "*A Piano For Mrs. Cimino* gives Bette Davis a shot at creating an individual. That's Davis' forté, as she's been proving for nearly half a century; now she can add Esther Cimino to her gallery." The New York *Times* agreed: "Miss Davis plays Mrs. Cimino with reserve, intelligence and suitable irascibility, and her initial senility is convincing too."

BELOW LEFT: Unexpectedly, Bette was in the news during the Summer of 1982—because of a casual remark she made in a magazine article. She mentioned that she had posed for a Boston sculptress when she was a teenager for a statue that was to represent Spring. She admitted that she had posed nude, and that the statue was now "in a park someplace in Boston." Within hours of the publication of the magazine piece, the "Great Bette Davis Statue Hunt" was launched.

Several statues were considered possibilities, including one that had stood in a fountain at the entrance of a city library but had been removed several years earlier because of public outcry about its "shamelessness." Finally, this piece—discovered in a back room of the Boston Museum of Fine Arts and entitled *Young Diana*—was decided upon because, according to researcher Florence Wolsky, "The statue's unusually expressive face, with its large eyes, does look much like a youthful Bette Davis."

BELOW RIGHT: Fifty years after they had first enjoyed evenings at the Coconut Grove nightclub, Bette and Ginger Rogers returned to the historic Hollywood spot in 1982 and posed following the presentation of The American Movie Award to Davis in honor of her lifetime of achievement. There was talk at this time of Ginger and Bette appearing on stage together for a benefit at the Olympia Theater in Paris, but this appearance never materialized.

OPPOSITE: Davis evokes the grandeur of an earlier age in this pose from *Little Gloria...Happy At Last*, another two-part television film that was shown on NBC on October 24 and 25, 1982. Based on the best-selling book by Barbara Goldsmith, *Little Gloria* traces the turbulent early years of millionairess Gloria Vanderbilt. Davis played the dominating matriarch Alice Gwynne Vanderbilt, and she joined a cast that included Angela Lansbury, Christopher Plummer, Maureen Stapleton and Glynis Johns. Bette's formidable character dies at the close of the first episode, but her presence is felt even during the proceedings of the story's second installment.

Variety's review of the saga was mixed: "Getting a look at all those pearls, fishknives and furs, and watching Bette Davis get a shot at being imperious again probably makes the venture amusing; but the telefilm with its awkward exposition and sensationalism...pokes around in lots of areas that seem better left undusted." The excellence of Bette's performance resulted in a Supporting Actress Emmy nomination.

TOP RIGHT: February 1983: Bette and her escort Roddy McDowall share a laugh as they pose for photographers at Twentieth Century-Fox studios, where they will be attending a lavish banquet in honor of visiting Queen Elizabeth II.

Less than two weeks later, Davis declared, "I've never felt so proud about being an American!" following still another honor: the Defense Department's highest award for a civilian for her efforts in founding the Hollywood Canteen during World War II. On hand to congratulate Bette are Martha Raye, wearing the numerous military decorations she has been awarded for her tireless entertainment efforts in Vietnam, and the much-honored Bob Hope.

This was surely the season of appreciating a living legend; Bette was receiving honors practically on a daily basis. Mayor Tom Bradley declared April 3, 1982 as officially Bette Davis Day in Los Angeles; she received a lifetime achievement award from the Film Advisory Board; the National Film Society presented her with that organization's first Golden Reel trophy, and she and Burt Reynolds were recipients of Valentino Awards, given by

a group of Rudolph Valentino admirers who annually salute the careers of enduring stars.

Bette realized a career-long dream when she signed to appear with James Stewart in the HBO cable television production *Right of Way*, about an unusual elderly couple, Teddy and Minnie Dwyer, who decide to commit suicide together when they learn that Minnie is terminally ill. Following filming in the Fall of 1982, Stewart and Davis talked with the press about working together for the first time in their lengthy, illustrious professional lives. "I'd have given anything to have met when we were younger," Bette admitted. "He didn't marry until late, 41 I think; if we had worked together before that I'd have *leapt* at him. First of all, I would have liked him because he is a very nice man. Then, he is also a wonderful actor. It would be hard to admire someone who is not a good actor."

Stewart, in his low-key manner, kept his comments confined to the film: "I liked it so much I would have done the project even if Bette and I had hated each other." Director George Schaefer added, "When you consider the contrasts in their acting styles, they meshed amazingly well." Davis felt that there was no noticeable difference. "I never felt out of sync with Jimmy," she said. "People think he is slow and I am fast, but the important thing is, he's a consummate actor who is always honest." Stewart agreed: "I never thought there was a contrast." *Right Of Way* was filmed on a $2.8-million budget in less than a month. When Bette was asked if the short shooting schedule had been difficult for her, she replied characteristically, "Why, I made a picture with Pat O'Brien called *Hell's House*, that we completed in one week. Of course, the picture looked like the title."

OPPOSITE: Bette as Miniature Dwyer, so named by her mother because of the miniature doll houses she was building when Minnie was born. When a social worker calls on the Dwyers to try and discuss their joint suicide intentions, she comments, "That's an unusual name"—to which Minnie responds, "I'm an unusual woman." And so she is. She approaches her impending death with a detached sense of practicality. She makes sure the dolls she has been making for years find proper homes, and she refuses to allow her emotionally-shattered daughter (Melinda Dillon) to interfere with her carefully thought-out plans to

end her life with her husband.

It is precisely this pragmatic quality that kept *Right Of Way* from really touching audiences. Teddy and Minnie are peculiar without being colorfully eccentric, and their decision to die together seems *too* well planned, allowing for little sentimentality. Even the scene of the actual suicide when they are sitting in the family car waiting for the carbon monoxide to take effect is strangely unmoving. The fault must lie with playwright Richard Lee's script, as Davis and Stewart could not be better within the confines of their roles as written. *Right Of Way* debuted over the HBO cable system during the summer of 1983, and disappointed those who were expecting an *On Golden Pond* type of entertainment.

After years of appearing in failed pilots, Bette signed on for a TV series that seemed destined for huge success—*Hotel*, based loosely on Arthur Hailey's popular novel. Joining cast members James Brolin and Connie Sellecca, pictured here, Davis (portraying chic hotel owner Laura Trent) began filming the show in April 1983. She made it clear, however, that her participation in *Hotel* would be limited to no more than nine episodes per season: "I think the way people in series work, 12-14 hours a day—well, they're killing themselves."

Sadly, after filming just two episodes, Bette became suddenly, dreadfully ill. In June, she underwent a mastectomy at New York Hospital-Cornell Medical Center. Her recovery from the surgery was complicated when she suffered a stroke. She fought back from both catastrophic illnesses, and was back home in West Hollywood by the end of the year.

Her recovery was progressing nicely when she fell and suffered a hip injury. At this writing, Bette is reportedly completely healed. She has kept a low public profile only because she wants her first interviews to concentrate on her return to acting, rather than on the multiple illnesses she has recently triumphed over.

Even without Bette, *Hotel* did become an enormous hit, but Davis decided not to return to the series. She has worked out her contract obligations with producer Aaron Spelling by agreeing to star in a TV movie in exchange for her release from *Hotel*.

OPPOSITE: In one of her last public appearances before her illnesses, Bette accepted this Best Actress trophy from the International Television Festival in Monte Carlo for her performance in *A Piano for Mrs. Cimino*.

It might be tempting for Bette Davis, after fifty years of acclaim—and struggle—to settle into a comfortable retirement. But she shows no interest in that option. She retains her youthful enthusiasm for her craft, and how it might stretch her talent. Indeed, her future holds new challenges. It was announced in October 1984 that Davis will costar for

the first time with Helen Hayes in a movie for CBS entitled *Murder With Mirrors*. And she has also expressed interest in starring in a mini-series about the colorful life of cosmetics queen Helena Rubinstein.

Bette Davis has proven herself again and again as a woman of tremendous resilience—both personally and professionally. If one thing may be said about her without fear of contradiction, it is that Bette Davis' talent is exceeded only by her guts.

PHOTO CREDITS

ABOUT THE AUTHOR

Christopher Nickens is the author of *Elizabeth Taylor: A Biography In Photographs*, and co-author of *The Telephone Book*. He collaborated with James Spada on the best-selling *Streisand: The Woman and the Legend*. He also recently illustrated the memoirs of Anne Francis, *Voices From Home*, and for five years served as Editor of *Barbra Quarterly*.

Mr. Nickens attended Hollywood High School and Cooper Union University in New York. He resides in his hometown of Los Angeles, and is currently at work on a pictorial biography of Natalie Wood.